100 Modern Soundtracks

100 MODERN SOUNDTRACKS

BFI Screen Guides

Philip Brophy

 Publishing

First published in 2004 by the
British Film Institute
21 Stephen Street, London W1T 1LN

The British Film Institute promotes greater understanding and appreciation of, and access to, film and moving image culture in the UK.

Cover design: Paul Wright
Cover image: *The Conversation* (Francis Ford Coppola, 1974, © Paramount Pictures Corporation)
Series design: Ketchup/couch
Set by Fakenham Photosetting Ltd, Fakenham, Norfolk
Printed in the UK by The Cromwell Press, Trowbridge, Wiltshire

British Library Cataloguing-in-Publication Data
A catalogue record for this book is available from the British Library

ISBN 1–84457–014–2 (pbk)
ISBN 1–84457–013–4 (hbk)

Contents

Acknowledgments

Thanks go to: Andrew Lockett for commissioning this thoroughly a-literate book; Adrian Martin for continual and ongoing encouragement and feedback on my writing on film sound and music; Rod Bishop and Les Walkling for allowing me to develop my Soundtrack courses over the years at RMIT Media Arts, plus my hyperactive take-no-shit students; Paul Schutze and Alessio Cavallaro for enabling publishing of my work; Tony Herrington at The Wire for allowing me to develop the 'Secret History of Film Music' series; Keith Gallasch and Virgina Baxter at Real Time for allowing me to develop the 'Cinesonic' series; all the amazing guests who attended the Cinesonic international conferences on film scores and sound design, plus my key staff – Megan Spencer, Emma Bortignon, Scott Goodings, Monica Zetlin, Adam Milburn; and producers and directors who have allowed me to put my ideas into practice on their films and projects – Lizzette Atkins, Rod Bishop, David Cox, Marie Craven, John Cruthers, Fiona Eagger, Tanya Hill, Vince Giarrusso, Ana Kokkinos, Aida Innocente, Daniel Scharf, Ilana Schulman, Sarah Zadeh, Lynne B. Williams, Monica Zetlin.

Introduction

Chimera cinema

Welcome to a vital component of the cinematic experience: the *soundtrack*. An awkward realm where grand symphonies collide with overhead helicopters in panoramic spectacle; a bloodied field where composers and sound designers come to blows during the final mix; a deep pit of disinformation from which are echoed truisms like 'modern movies are too noisy', 'only orchestras can produce quality music', 'film sound should be natural', 'film music works best when you don't notice it', and 'the art of movies died with the coming of sound'.

Clearly, the soundtrack is a chimera of the cinema. It is sound *and* noise; noise *and* music; music *and* speech; speech *and* sound. At no point can it be distilled into a form which allows us to safely state its essential quality. The soundtrack is a world caught in eternal disequilibrium by two meta-forces: *film scores* – the commissioned composition of music for specific scenes – and *sound design* – the conceptualisation of how dialogue, sound effects and atmospheres are edited and mixed to provide the sound for a scene. Despite the many existing ways in which critics and practitioners tend to *separate* the two forces, they continue to combine according to a unique, mutative and hermetic logic – little of which conforms to literary models, operatic figures, painterly diagrams or photographic allusions. In order to accept this inability of sound and music to be essenced from each other, one has to think with one's ears.

The cinesonic womb

Sonic beings at our deepest and most unconscious level, we are shaped by sonar and aquatic sensations well before we are birthed into air and light. The sensorium of the womb is our primary induction into sound. The curvaceous film theatre returns us directly to a psycho-physical zone of uterine impressions: deep rumbles, pink noise, shifting timbres, spatial reflections, swelling rhythms. Much has been made of the cinema as some sort of primordial social cave for storytelling. The cinema is a *womb* where the sonic prevails.

We say we 'watch' movies, but the 'cinesonic' experience is far more than a mere optical event. Try watching a film with no sound: gone is its power, emotion, drama, vitality. Shut your eyes and listen to the soundtrack, and through the blackness one can be excited by the orchestration of voices, atmospheres, effects and music. This is how the sonic engulfs us in the unfolding audiovisual carnival that is the cinema.

Yet like a mysterious hieroglyphic stream, those squiggly white lines to the left of the celluloid film strip lay silent even to the inquiring eye – under-theorised, presumed unimportant, yet vital to the history of audiovisuality, and integral to technological advances in the entertainment industries over the past twenty-five years. You know this without realising it. But thanks to years of optical and literal orientation, you articulate filmic experience through words which use visual metaphors. Though after a few simple pointers about how sound works, the most complex issues of the soundtrack's narrative power can become remarkably evident.

Planet sound

This book will guide you through the audiovisual layering of a wide range of films, as eclectic in their collection as they are essential in their status. Instead of forcing these varied movies into a pre-fab mould for ascribing significance, they are discussed to demonstrate how they *shoot us back into the noise of reality* – into its psychological sonorum which affects our everyday sense of time, space, mass, force, presence. The first bird of morning, a distant siren at midnight, a woman's scream next door, your baby's giggle, the last breath of your dying father, that inopportune phone ring, that heavenly voice – these are not mere 'sound effects' to you or me. Nor do they ever behave so in a film.

Night clubs, the ocean, tunnels, elevator muzak, stadium concerts, shopping malls, Walkmans, home theatres, subway PAs, forests, freeways, televisions in the next room while we eat breakfast – we are surrounded by sonic spaces. You have experienced all this – but little has been said about how cinema revives and reworks these temperate aural realities which direct your everyday momentum.

Braille for the deaf

In an attempt to move away from many well-applied literary and visual frameworks through which the cinema has been perceived, *structural models of meaning* are disavowed in favour of *flow charts of effects*. Following the voluminous ways in which sound and music become manifest, every film covered in the book is treated primarily as a *spatio-temporal* event whose movement, denouement and performance is cited and noted for its audiovisual impact. Fundamentally, this requires a different mode of writing whose 'flow' is more important in its capture, replay and rendering of a film's momentum, than it is in summarising, reducing or even encapsulating a film's signifying skeleton. A kind of 'Braille for the deaf' is required.

While many 'classics of cinema' are absent from this book, its focus on the complexity of the soundtrack uncovers that the more interesting and engrossing films may not be those missing 'classics', but those whose soundtracks psychologically excite the auditory membrane. The ultimate aim of this book is to induce a *consciousness* of how the soundtrack operates on what we presume to be our perceptual facilities for comprehending film.

Diagnosing the modern

All 100 entries move forward from the view that *modernism* is destruction: a decimation of all that has naturally grown by itself. Cinema is a *spectacular practice* of this destruction: Frankensteinian in its assemblage, Futurist in its bombast. All that is modern in cinema is the result of technological, metaphysical and existential inquiry. Cinema's modern audiovisuality therefore has less to do with the enlightened Classical arts of literature, theatre, painting – even music; it has more to do with endoscopic exploration, plastic surgery, chemical alteration, electroshock therapy and nerve stimulation. And when cinema does appear to be natural, Romantic, Classical – that's when it's at its most artificial, most inhuman, most unreal.

This book is thus concerned with, swayed by and attracted to cinema which exhibits the scars, make-up and covering of these operations upon its corpus, and whose soundtracks acknowledge the mutated state of being which arises from decentred and deconstructed audiovisual distribution. These are the films that are textually filtrated with the voices of Glenn Gould, Phil Spector, Luigi Russolo, John Cage, Roland Barthes, Link Wray, Erik Satie, Kraftwerk, Yoko Ono, Harry Partch, Jimi Hendrix and Karlheinz Stockhausen, among others. While this brethren may not appear to be directly connected to the cinema, enough films have been made in the last century to form a complex webbing to their work and philosophies so as to constitute a sizeable body nominated herewith as 'the modern soundtrack'.

Threaded throughout this book's films are the key transformations by which the modern soundtrack is manifest:

(i)   ruminations on the nature of recorded sound;

(ii)   the bombastic deployment of sound effects;

(iii)   the spatialisation of atmospheres and environments;

(iv)   orchestral collapses and interiorisations;

(v)   celebrations of electricity;

(vi)   the weaving and threading of songs; and

(vii) the processing of vocal grain.

A brief discussion of each of these technical and symbolic manoeuvres follows.

The nature of sound

Sound has many layers to its manifestation. While established discourses enable separation and focus to perceive how sound occurs, it is only on the film soundtrack that all the conflicting discourses of sound are uncontrollably collided.

Basic layers of sound would be the *physical* – how sound moves through air and other substances; the *neurological* – how sound is received by the ear and processed by the brain; the *psychological* – how sound is perceived, interpreted and associated with the self, its emotional state and its mental composure. Note how these basic layers virtually form a linear pathway from event to reception to comprehension, each with its territorial break-away path hightailing it back to subsets of the sciences.

But sound has other routes which can cross, overpass or merge with the above rationalist triangulation. A secondary set of layers would be the *psychoacoustic* – how the physics of sound are irrevocably tied to the conditions of listening and the mental adjustment to sound's situation; the *phonological* – how sound is reconstructed in the acts of recording, encoding and rendering; and the *performative* – how sound as an event unfolds and reveals itself as gesture, occurrence and shape.

Whenever sound occurs in conjunction with image, its status cannot be qualified, described or annotated by any one layer of our cinesonic sextet outlined above. Issues of physical reality, personal memories, interpretative reading and aural appreciation will be invoked in the attempt to digest such an event. And yet the audiovisual event will remain fraught with mystery: is it a statement? a documentation? a symbol? an incision? a dimension?

Modern soundtracks are those that illustrate either a *single* heightened sensation of one of these layers – as an act of artificial rupture and dislocation, considering that all six modulate and affect each other in differing proportion – or an *overload* of all layers – as a demonstration of sound's ability to overcome and obliterate. The 'nature of sound' in this sense is not a/any/all sound's essential or absolute guise (as such divination is impossible) but its irrefutable behaviour, distinctive apparition and ingrained purpose. It eschews any essence as to what it might be – as if it is a metaphor pointing to some sonic soul that has motivated the act of description – and instead accepts its pliability, malleability and flexibility as its power.

The nature of sound is thus overtly coded and transmitted as a self-reflexive act in *The Conversation* (1974), where an audio surveillance specialist becomes so obsessed with a particular recording that his world is transformed. *Blue* (1993) contains no images bar a blue screen, yet its soundtrack is used as an intensely personal 'sonic diary'. The nature of sound can be constituted as an amplified stream of erotica as in *Temptress Moon* (1996), or it can be a debilitating shell-shock embodying familial discord, as in *The Straight Story* (1999). All these discrete manifestations and more are each their own exemplar, their own evidence of the nature of sound.

The bombast of effects

For some, sound in the cinema is a form of noise pollution, as if its energy is overbearing, dominating and numbing. This has formed the basis for arguing that cinema's audiovisual loudness is some awful pop culture noise constituting an unnecessary interference to the artful act of communicating cinematically. For others, film sound is the welcomed 'bombast of effects' which cinema uniquely delivers.

In the realm of the modern soundtrack, this is where sound may appear to be an attack on the audience. Far from it: sound is hurled, jettisoned and directed at the audience only in order to figure how sound can *resonate* with the body of the viewer; how sound itself can attain a *bodily presence* which sets up a sensational dialogue with our bodies and minds.

This is where *animism* overrides humanism, in testament to sound's transformative power and its extant energy. Sound energises the space between that which is broadcast and that which is received, thereby maximising the act of listening (in the Cageian sense) and quelling any notion that intaking film entails a contract of passive consumption. The bombast of effects states that sound comes from the screen not in an act of 'describing' what the screen holds, but in an act of becoming itself, of coming alive. This constitutes an entirely different operation from 'reading', 'understanding' or 'deciphering' the 'meaning of sound'. Sound's bombast on the modern soundtrack is authorless and inhuman, yet directional and affecting.

When this sonic animism intersects with and modulates the human drama which propels the bulk of storytelling in the cinema, the former does not preclude or negate the latter. If anything, a heightened humanism can be expressed when one accepts the base power of sound as something greater than the fictionalised personages and imagined psyches which populate the cinema. Modern soundtracks which take this recourse in their sound design and mixage generate awe-inspiring results, opening up the cinema to broader statements of life.

Hyper thrillers like *Angel Dust* (1995) and unclassifiable pornography like *Beneath the Valley of the Ultra-Vixens* (1979) certainly bombard the audience with a barrage of psycho-sexual blips, glitches, gulps and groans – but in order to analyse audience response to unsettling modes of sexual exchange. Science-mysteries like *The Birds* (1963) and wild cartoons like *Guided Muscle* (1955) form massed attacks on the audience with alienating noise and explosive sonics – but in order to symbolise the subjective viewpoints of their characters' tribulations. And films like *M* (1931) and *The Innocents* (1961) zone in on the audience to conduct experiments on them with great subtlety and precision – but in the process generate a chillingly distilled cinema on par with the most bombastic.

The marvel of space

Somewhere between the death of live musical accompaniment to so-called silent cinema and the wide application of Dolby surround sound in theatres, the soundtrack lay *spatially* dormant. That is, whatever 'space' was signified by any on-screen or off-screen sound was technologically and ontologically streamed from the front-on emission of the screen.

This, however, was a tenuous negation of all that defines sound according to laws of physics. You need space for sound to occur, and sound can only be manifest through agent, action and auditor coexisting in a shared or correlated space. Sound and music that surround us in the everyday are mostly detached from the scopic. This tends towards a split between the *consciousness of sound* – that impelled by acts of listening, notions of importance and relevance, and objects of aural desire – and its *unconsciousness* – that requiring only the slightest act of hearing, placing sound as backgrounded, unfocused, diffused, ambienced.

Cinema has had to build upon its soundtrack a complete restructuring of the networking between the sonically conscious and the aurally unconscious. Film scores and sound design would be two historical crafts and industrial operations which contribute to this, developing myriad ways that manipulate the audience into simulated shifts between the conscious and unconscious. While categorical recognition of all that is not-music (i.e. sound) and all that is not-sound (i.e. music) is the prime and somewhat narrowing linguistic purpose of film audiovision, identification of location, direction and space must also be controlled while the audience is fixed on staring at a screen in front of them.

The movie screen psycho-optically suggests not only a window onto the world but also the feeling of being trapped in a black box. You are deprived of even the base power of sight you have when you choose to idly look out a window; your view is held, changed, designed beyond your will. The 'marvel of space' arises from your sitting in isolation in the cinema's black box, subjected to an array of sounds, many of which have no direct relation to that which appears on the screen. Not only do various types of sounds appear gratuitously, illogically, irrationally, they also shift through the black space which engulfs you. You are excited and terrified by that which is beyond the perimeters of the screen and that which sounds behind you.

When perceived in this way, the modern soundtrack is in no way a slave in service to the image: film sound/music moulds a key for realigning our consciousness to a non-hierarchical order of the senses.

We might not have eyes in the back of our heads, but our ears can hear everything behind our head as well as all that is in front of our eyes. The modern soundtrack delights in rejoining actualised space to projected image – to lever listening over seeing – either symbolically as in *House By The River* (1950) and *Stalker* (1979); cosmologically as in *Close Encounters of the Third Kind* (1977) and *Contact* (1997); or technologically as in *Lost Highway* (1997) and *Cast Away* (2000).

The collapse of the orchestra

The swirling sonic grandeur of a symphony orchestra is considered to be a sign of 'production value' for many cinemagoers – so much so that the orchestra's harmonic richness typifies 'the sound of film music'. Innumerable film scores feature a bellowing orchestra echoing the cavernous majesty of Richard Wagner and the acidic sweetness of Richard Strauss. Certainly, film music can reference these composers' work, and do so with imagination and verve. But there are other options.

There have been a number of rebukes of how orchestral beauty and grandeur had been envisioned and employed in the preceding four centuries. Composers-cum-theorists who enabled this in the first half of the 20th century (Arnold Schoenberg, Igor Stravinsky, Béla Bartók, Edgar Varèse, Anton Webern, Pierre Boulez, Iannis Xenakis, Kryzsztof Penderecki, Olivier Messiaen and György Ligeti to name a few) collectively reimagined, reinvented and reconfigured the orchestra as a new compositional apparatus and sound-generating machine, while using the materials, methods and meanings endeared by preceding centuries' rationale of orchestral composition.

The technological democratisation of the soundtrack – where all becomes abstractly sonic despite its linguistic crafting – should have welcomed the cinematised orchestra to be rendered more akin to the modernist techniques of the aforementioned avant-garde composers. But it has remained a withering pursuit in the rigidly codified terrain of the film score. There, a reduced emotional range is guarded by harmonic sentinels – the major and minor modes – who rationalise psychological nuance. Atonality is allowed on the film score mostly to signify the Other: the monstrous, the grotesque, the aberrant. Like the ultimate death which must befall the movie monster, the presence of atonality must be marked as transgressive and unforgiving. Far from being emancipated (as per Schoenberg's wish), dissonance is condemned.

While the storytelling impulses which crazily guide a populist movie may be rendered thin and shallow by classical notions of myth or the purist ideals of the avant-garde, those impulses are astounding when gauged by modern and post-modern audiovisual perception. Many a modern soundtrack vibrantly celebrates the collapse of the orchestra: from Bernard Herrmann's dissonant transsexuality in *Psycho* (1960) and de-jazzed asexuality in *Taxi Driver* (1976) to Toru Takemitsu's psychological soundscape in *Arashi ga oka* (1988) and pathological noise-quake in *Kaidan* (1964), the deeper inner power of the orchestral machine resonates boldly in the cinema.

The rise of electricity

In its amalgamation of the plastic arts, cinema never experiences a dilemma in foregrounding the painterly, the theatrical, the choreographic, the photographic or the acoustic. All these modes of depiction, their historical artistry and their specific disciplines are regarded as 'cinematic' when they are blended onto the screen. But what about the *electric*? Cinema that shows its electrical circuitry is generally unwanted despite its revelation of its technological being. A chemo-electrical medium if ever there was one, cinema is preferred to look photographic, sometimes concede to being theatrical, but always to sound acoustic. Yet the 'rise of electricity' on the modern soundtrack's film score breaks this aural ordinance via its unabashed display of *rock instrumentation* – where electricity connotes volume and vulgarity – and *electronic synthesisers* – where electricity connotes unhumanness and unnaturalism.

Evoking its lumpen weight and compacted form, the word 'rock' perfectly describes the granulitic, gravity-bearing power of a music predicated on volume, mass and density. No wonder it has been granted scant environmental hold in the shimmering, flickering world of cinema and its ghostly evocation of wispy imagery. Historically, cinema is a machine of the phantasmagorical: a play upon the fantastic evocation of impossible images and imaginable scenes. When rock music occurs on the film soundtrack, it smashes that arcana of slide projections and light shows with volcanic force. The air becomes thick and sound degenerates into noise – reminding us that hidden behind the silver screen's porous fabric are *speakers*.

While rock was spawned by the horizontal spread of the recording industry, synthesisers have grown from the vertical sprout of the electronic academy. This, however, has not ensured it a lofty perch within cinema; quite the opposite, the extremities of its electrification have garnered it a most remote address. Electronics – taking in everything from unpitched oscillators and tone generators and over-reverberant clangs and scrapes, to googly bleeps of electrified fakeness and synthesisers emulating strings, choirs and flutes – are pictured as android when they touch any other sonic or musical element on the film soundtrack. But this is the seductive charm of synthesisers: they can do the one thing humans cannot do – be inhuman.

Fortunately, historical slivers of rock-scoring and synth-scoring trail across the body of cinema like barely visible scars. From screaming theremins in Russian sci-fi of the 50s to fuzzed guitars in American biker movies of the 60s to wailing organs in Italian and French sex movies of the 70s to sequenced synthesisers in MTV-styled crime movies of the 80s, the underbelly of cinema is tattooed with all manner of rock, funk and electronica. Recording studio productions predicated on fuzz, wah and echoplex – *Suspiria* (1977), *Teenage Rebellion* (1967), *Shaft* (1971) – experiments in amplified form for cinema out-on-a-limb – *Dead Man* (1995), *Rumble Fish* (1983), *Sympathy for the Devil* (1968) – and monstrous reconstructions of that which purists cannot even call music – *Forbidden Planet* (1954), *Escape from New York* (1981), *Scarface* (1983).

The fabric of song

An unfortunate elitism places song at the peripheries of music's artistry, as if song's ephemeral, transitory and disposable nature discounts meaning, significance or statement. Opera is allowed song – but via the pure and controlled streaming of known mythological shapes through dramatic exposition. The 'phantom voicing' of the libretto is replicated in the bulging diaphragms of its singers whose contralto implies that the purity of their un-breathed tone allows 'pure' musical narrative form to be annunciated spiritually.

In the more common sense, song is the noise of the crowd: authorless per citation, but 'authorful' per density of reference and spread of relevance. Song is an expression of the vernacular, the vulgar, the vocal; and like a healthy breeding unit, it facilitates the production of more song. Class associations with this notion of song have for centuries relegated it to the lower domains of culture, as its lack of rarefaction qualifies it full of impurity. Songs in film have long been cited by a wide range of cultures and historical periods as a wet blanket for the artistically enlightened and a succulent teat for popular audiences. The dawn of cinema – up to and through the entrenchment of sound cinema – was a rowdy populist din echoing the market noise of Tin Pan Alley, desperate to employ song to characterise, identify and commodify the new technological industry of entertainment.

Song, therefore, wears its origins loudly and distastefully as far as most film aesthetes are concerned. But this is irony of a high order, for the core of the disrecognition of song is the assumption of it being form – when it is *fabric*. Its patterning is the result of complex micro-structural activity, wherein overall effect arises from a less discernible organisation of collective energies. Film in this sense could be regarded as being more *song* than anything else: both exhibit this same formal multiplicity, compounded plasticity, and aggregated expression. Films emblazoned with modern soundtracks tend to be those which aspire to the condition of music generally, song especially. Their incorporation of the 'fabric of song' proceeds their knowledge of the power of song, allowing song primacy of place in their radiophonic narratives where story is not 'told' but more broadcast, transmitted and mixed.

Like a monstrously large warehouse of material, the fabric of song can contain many sheens, patterns and colours in its cinematic cut. *American Graffiti* (1973) uses songs of an epoch to transport one back in time not for evocation, but to plonk one down in the radiophonic terrain of the 60s. *The Ballad of Narayama* (1958) uses song to speak from a long and respectful lineage in kabuki theatre, where numerous side-narrations in song form are integral to the multi-faceted experience of its stories. *The Colour of Pomegranates* (1969) uses song in the archaic iconic tradition, referencing its propensity to frame the pre-musical domain of the lyrical, and to then poetically realise those shapes in cinematic guise. The list is as long as a song that never ends.

The grain of the voice

Speech is a particularly self-gratifying trait of humans. Amazed by our control of intellectual concepts and abstract language through words spoken and written, we confer respect and power upon those who articulate, narrate, dictate, orate. The power of speech, the control over language and the kingdom of the written all account for cinema's prioritisation of speech on the soundtrack.

Yet closer inspection of film speech reveals it rarely to be a voice, and mostly an aural stream of the written, where actors – as per stage dramaturgy – are empty vessels through which the words of the author are breathed. The advent of the soundtrack – initially discounted by conservatives – technologically empowered the archaic domain of theatre and its literary templates, even though theatre rejected cinema's modernism. Theatre needn't have worried: the recorded voice was as powerful a written edict as any legal declaration of literature's dictatorial regime. Speech – the manifestation of scripted dialogue – mostly roots cinema in the written and inures a deafness to the *spoken*: to the materiality of the voice, its fibrous utterance and its sensual frottage.

To rescue the cinematic voice from being muffled and muted by this conservatism requires the most extreme deprogramming of any of our cinesonic sextet of aural layers that define the modern soundtrack. Films which foreground the 'grain of the voice' have to resort to the most obtuse methods and uncompromising means, abstracting the voice as delivery to hold onto its physicality. The voice is an undeniably erotic and eroticised device. In cinema, it can be the aurally fragrant wisps of the siren, the orgasmic spluttering of bodies pushing themselves to the limit, the thigh-quivering roar of the omnipotent phallus, the stratospheric soars of the diva, the virginal ripeness of the pre-pubescent androgyne, the arousing maturity of the deep and husky crone. Further, these sexual modes can be conveyed through the exotic appeal and lure of a thick accent or an unknown language; the iconic drawl and familiar ring of a rich and fulsome identity; or the acoustic, electronic or digital distillation of timbrel colour and breath.

Modern soundtracks centred on the grain of the voice are either those that employ the voice not as a tool but as an *instrument*, or those that utilise speech not for content but for its *orchestration*. These streams – sometimes parallel, sometimes perpendicular, sometimes conjoined to each other – emanate from pre-literary or non-written realms: the confessional mutterings of the diaristic; the multiple identities of the schizophrenic; the suppressed expression of the traumatised; the misguided directives of the lovelorn; the screaming noise of the aberrant. Their vocal trajectory and non-vocal suction displace words and re-centre the act of speaking as a dramatic fulcrum to certain films' narrative purpose. *I Spit On Your Grave* (1978) and *Rosetta* (1999) generate a deafening and disturbing silence through the refusal of speech by their characters. *California Split* (1974) and *Dr. Dolittle* (1998) strike extremes of psychological disequilibrium through their cacophonous excess of speech. *Last Year at Marienbad* (1959) and *The Man Who Lies* (1968) treat voice as nothing but an unstoppable widening of the gulf which separates truth from all acts of inscription.

Troubleshooting

Why aren't there any musicals in this book? We are focused here on the modern soundtrack as (i) a multi-realm where sound, music, noise and speech repel and attract each other; (ii) a meta-terrain where all practical definitions of sound are collided; and (iii) a hyper-dimension where the becoming of sound overwhelms any separate cine-linguistic mode of expression. The conventions of the musical relate to pre-modern manifestations of the soundtrack which – with comparative comfort – facilitated and allowed forms of opera and theatre to be integrated into cinematic form. Classical Hollywood musicals would then be more documentaries than anything else in their cinematic assimilation of the spatial warp between the Broadway stage and the Hollywood soundstage. A separate book would better service 'the modern musical'.

Where are the auteurs in this book? Credits for each film appear at the bottom of each entry – but names are largely absent in the accompanying text. This is in recognition of sound's animist being – its pre- and post-human aura – which seizes the sonic senses with utmost embrace. When I hear helicopters and synthesisers swirl around me, infused in the stereo retreat and lurch of 'The End' in *Apocalypse Now* (1979), my mind is not picturing Coppola, Murch and Morrison as if their heads are carved in stone in front of the theatre speakers – even though sound designers and film composers comprise the artists and artisans for materialising the soundtrack. Each entry is focused on the sensorial, phenomenological and perceptual dynamism of the soundtrack discussed. The reader is invited to listen along these lines.

What can I do with this book? This book is not a manual for general use: it is designed to aid in perceiving these films of a peculiar sono-musical bent. You may not be able to 'apply' its ideas to something else. You might be able to find other films by the same director, composer and/or sound designer that have similar aspects and interests as those of their works cited here, but more likely than not there will be little correlation or continuity. The ideas in this book have grown directly from the films cited – each entry only touching on some of the film's pertinent cinesonic issues – and in no way preceded the films. Hyper-materialist in orientation, the assertion of this thing called 'the modern soundtrack' is a guide to itself; the films collectively comprise a map, but like a technological palimpsest, it needs to be continually rewritten.

Akira
Japan, 1988 – 124 mins
Katsuhiro Otomo

The character Tetsuo in *Akira* is a quintessential post-nuclear being.
Emblematic of the film's seminal cyberpunk themes, he is able to exist
beyond the putative constrictions of physical existence. He transforms
physically; he projects psychically; he transports himself between spatio-
temporal dimensions. Tetsuo's anger often erupts in a series of shock
waves, hurling balls of energy which emanate from his being and rupture
his surrounding physical surfaces like a ball pressed into clay.

The central physical agent and symbolic receptacle of energy in
Akira, Tetsuo makes his mark in ways analogous to sound: through a
series of waves, patterns and disturbances upon material surfaces. Cast
in a peculiarly Japanese physicality, his presence is like that of a

Akira: a cosmologically sonic film

calligrapher's brush on paper or a samurai's sword on flesh, all being symptomatic of channelling energy through the body to leave a mark of that energy's dispersion. This also happens to be the way in which sound manifests itself through air and upon surfaces.

Moving continually through these scales of materiality, *Akira* is a cosmologically sonic film. It positions all spaces and environments to capture recordings of energy waves and lines. Atomic bomb blasts leave huge craters downtown; an ESPer's piercing scream shatters glass buildings; psychic energy causes subterranean chambers to rise and rupture the overground. At its most extreme, the architecture of *Akira* is rendered not as solid form, but as a network of recordable surfaces. Logically, the soundtrack highlights how energy waves and lines perform in this manner by exploring the various ways that sound can be temporally split from image, for we most notice the effect of sound when it does not obey the constriction of image. In *Akira*, the sound of destruction is thus asynchronous. As a single percussive incident, it is mistimed to the visual moment of destruction; as an aural passage, it is delayed from the visual sequence of destruction.

When Kanada tries to shoot Tetsuo with a laser gun at the start of their final showdown in the empty stadium, Tetsuo hurls an energy ball towards him. As the veins build on his forehead in a spread of humoral tributaries, so does the concrete break up due to fault lines fanning out as if responding to an earthquake. The synchronous relation between the dynamic events is thus delayed, extended and established as a running counterpoint to the visual action.

When the SOL satellite beam is first sent down to the stadium, the audiovisual delays in the Kanada–Tetsuo fight are transformed into a complete dislocation between sound and image. The atmosphere becomes enveloped by a bright blue haze; a deadly silence befalls the scene; a thin ray of light appears; gravity is altered as small pebbles slowly rise. Then the soundtrack erupts in a series of explosions as the ground is carved up by the beam like a gigantic samurai sword slicing across concrete. In response to this audiovisual rupture, Tetsuo beams himself up past the threshold of earth's atmosphere. There in the silence of space, he rips apart the satellite. Visual explosions appear, but the soundtrack is dead silent. On numerous occasions in *Akira*, the most devastating destruction comes from energy so intense it appropriately appears to be beyond the recording range of the soundtrack.

Dir: Katsuhiro Otomo; **Prod:** Shunzo Kato, Ryohei Suzuki; **Scr:** Katsuhiro Otomo, Izo Hashimoto; **DOP:** Katsuji Misawa; Editor: Takeshi Seyama; **Score:** Shoji Yamashiro; **Sound Recording Director:** Susumu Akitagawa; **Sound Effects Supervisor:** Shizuo Kusahashi; **Sound Recording Supervisor:** Tetsuo Segawa; **Sound Recording Architect:** Keiji Urata; **Voice Cast:** Mitsuo Iwata, Nozomu Sasaki, Mami Koyama, Tessho Genda.

American Graffiti
US, 1973 – 110 mins
George Lucas

While memories least accord to chronological and linear organisation in their recall, their selective use in movie 'flashbacks' forces them into determined sequences, usually to withhold information as much as convey it. *American Graffiti* employs a 'social flashback' by casting its narrative into the past and asking its audience to remember the era: 'Where were you in '62?'

Yet in contrast to the ellipses and fragmentation which normally occur during flashbacks, *American Graffiti*'s events are synced to slabs of real-time radio broadcast on the last night of summer vacation in California's suburban Valley in 1962. The early 60s was a major transition of radio consumption in America, moving from the family-rooted living-room fixture of its aural hearth, to multi-market points of multiplied reception, resulting from public address systems in drive-through premises and transistor and car radios of newly mobile teenagers. *American Graffiti* captures a sonic landscape of how radio was broadcast in this epoch, through a cartographic overview of the teenagers' movements from school to burger joints to hops to drive-ins to lovers' lanes. As we follow them through these spaces, we audition stark contrasts in the acoustic toning of each environment, feeling the echoic spread in parking lots and the compressed tinny quality of hand-held transistors.

Within this articulated sonar field, famous songs by Buddy Holly, Chuck Berry and others do not simply replace film score, nor do they merely provide historical contextualisation for the film. Due to their acoustic rendering throughout *American Graffiti*, they serve as a base terrain that maps teenage mobility. As a forecast of so-called 'short attention spans', the editing of *American Graffiti* generates a set of synaptic jumps within any one song's objective whole: the song's form continues the cycling of its verse/chorus pleasure principle, while aspects and angles of the form are fractured in sonic cubism courtesy of greater Los Angeles' architecture and urban design.

Plot momentum and direction rejoin this aural thematic as Curt's (Dreyfuss) attraction to the radio DJ (who creates a community of kids through his rock'n'roll broadcast) leads him to station XERB. There we meet none other than Wolfman Jack (an original DJ from the era now playing himself some years on). Regarded as a 'voice' of Curt's generation, his role within *American Graffiti* is as sage to Curt's dawning search for meaning. *American Graffiti*'s subtextual implication of rock'n'roll songs being the source of greater meaning which require one's journey of discovery within their corridors is refreshingly respectful of pop and music.

Dir: George Lucas; **Prod:** Francis Ford Coppola, Gary Kurtz; **Scr:** George Lucas, Gloria Katz, Willard Huyck; **DOP:** Jan D'Alquen, Ron Eveslage; **Editor:** Verna Field, George Lucas, Maria Lucas; **Songs:** includes Bill Haley and the Comets, Chuck Berry, Buddy Holly, the Beach Boys, Del Shannon, Frankie Lymon and the Teenagers, the Platters, the Diamonds, Joey Dee and the Starlighters, the Big Bopper, Fats Domino, Bobby Freeman, Johnny Burnette, the Clovers, Booker T. and the MGs; **Sound Design:** Walter Murch; **Main Cast:** Richard Dreyfuss, Ron Howard, Paul Le Mat, Charles Martin Smith, Cindy Williams, Candy Clark, Wolfman Jack.

Angel Dust (*Enjeru dasuto*)
Japan, 1995 – 117 mins
Sogo Ishii

It is near impossible to separate *Angel Dust*'s sound design from its film score. This aural puzzle is in part a reconstruction of the film's Möbius strip of thriller and mystery devices. A thriller envelope is shaped by the Tokyo police in pursuit of a serial killer injecting women with poison every Monday at 6 p.m. on the subway. A mystery envelope evolves when they enlist psychiatrist Setsuko Suma (Minami) who seeks help from her teacher Dr Rei Aku (Wakamatsu), who in turn may be responsible for creating the serial killer following some experimental deprogramming he conducted on radical cult members some years earlier.

Wavering between an objective compiling of facts and the subjective state of being mentally deprogrammed, *Angel Dust*'s fusion of sound design and film score constitutes a delicate yet assaulting collage of musical fragments which hurtle, jettison and freeze mid-air throughout the film like a series of alien objects. These score 'objects' are arranged as pre-composed pieces savagely excerpted, cross-faded and inserted as glimpses on one's aural periphery. No cues, no passages, no sections. Only a broad band radiation of textures which signifies the presence of musicality without advancing any music; like a live broadcast of the soundtrack received by wildly flicking tuner dials on a bank of radios. Music comes and goes, leaving one more conscious of its presence and absence than its content; more massaged by the extremities of its frequency range than by its formal orchestration.

In its frenetic editing and mixing, *Angel Dust* invokes a highly materialist concept of the electronic globe: a sono-musical appreciation of information technologies as opposed to immaterial ideas of global media convergence. *Angel Dust* actively sounds this idea as it sculpts noise, paints tones and casts timbres in reflection of its post-nuclear environment, giving us a rush of shivers, spasms and stabs in the name of music. Its soundtrack is the result of extending our currently saturated noise-fields so bemoaned by 'acoustic ecologists' around the world. *Angel Dust* actively refutes the simplistic negative connotations of noise and instead reads noise as the gateway to fluid, elusive and redefining notions of how sound floats around us, bombards us, tricks us and responds to us. The cat-and-mouse game carried out by Setsuko and Dr Aku sets up a psychological grid positioned in the contemporary noise-field of Tokyo's metropolis of rumbling subways, reverberant corridors, and rhythmic escalators; the hyperactive cut-and-paste of its sonic details is crucial to capturing the sound of modern life.

Bathed in the cold green haze of fluorescent tubing, *Angel Dust*'s cinematography at times mimics a video aesthetic – a taste usually repelled by film's so-called 'warmth'. The look of the film is thus a refusal of its presumed identity, and imitates the sound design and film score's replication of the other's form, shape and presence. The resulting audiovisual hall of sonic mirages plays its own cat-and-mouse game with the audience, as harmonious discord and tempered dissonance reflect a Japanese philosophical acceptance of how beauty and ugliness are at one with the other.

Dir: Sogo Ishii; **Prod:** Kenzo Horikoshi, Eiji Izumi, Taro Maki; **Scr:** Yorozu Ikuta, Sogo Ishii; **DOP:** Norimichi Kasamatsu; **Editor:** Sogo Ishii, Hiroshi Matsuo; **Score:** Hiroyuki Nagashima; **Sound Recording:** Nobuyuki Kikuchi; **Main Cast:** Kaho Minami, Takeshi Wakamatsu, Etsushi Toyokawa, Ryoko Takizawa.

Apocalypse Now
US, 1979 – 153 mins
Francis Ford Coppola

The Vietnam era has been historically mediarised as a McLuhanesque rupture of the domestic by the electronic image (televised images with little location sound and maximal voiceover reportage), leaving us to presume that the sonic, the acoustic, the spatial and the psychoacoustic had no role to play in 'Nam and interventionist conflicts around the globe since. *Apocalypse Now* is arguably a 'self-mediarised text' in its knowing relation to the sociology of images, yet the rigour with which it pays attention to sound is notable. The film was influenced and guided by documentary film-maker Eugene S. Jones, who supplied detailed sono-spatial notes on just about every piece and component of weaponry and ammunition used in the Vietcong field and jungle conflicts. The in-the-field experience of Jones aided in forming a valuable aural topology for *Apocalypse Now*.

Yet *Apocalypse Now*'s 'reality effect' – much touted and cited by cinema critics and the film's crew alike – runs counter to the psychological portraiture with which the film primarily grapples. Enmeshed in the contracting psychic space of Captain Willard (Sheen) at a mental precipice, and Colonel Kurtz (Brando) lost in a black hole of paranoia, *Apocalypse Now* creates a composite study of the points of impact which guarantee post-war shock. Via Willard's ride down the chopper-laden vertebrae of the Doors' 'The End' to the dark cave of Kurtz's murmured invocation of Joseph Conrad's *Heart of Darkness*, we recognise psyches that still reverberate, rack, shudder and flinch with psychoacoustic replays of military 'noisefare' encoded into their being and looped into uncontrollable and unpredictable cycles of playback and feedback. As much a defiant veteran reclamation as an anguished anti-war statement, *Apocalypse Now* renders sound as terror. It knows that that bomb blast you survived haunts you with every loud slam of a car door; that rocket launch whoosh you dodged taunts you with every buffet of wind through overhead power lines. From the actual sonic event in the past, to its acoustic resemblance in the present, to its imaginary recall in one's mind, all sounds can trigger the same disorienting asynchronism advanced by the audiovisual dislocation in war.

The original quadraphonic and later surround sound mixes of *Apocalypse Now* promote this notion that war is noise. Tactical land warfare reconfigures space as an amplified terrain of threatening sonic occurrences whose indistinction and multiplicity confer sound as noise – as a complete collapse of decipherable sound. *Apocalypse Now* exemplifies this by cataloguing everything from faint rustles in the bush

Apocalypse Now: war as the ultimate dislocation of sound from image

to simulated bird calls in the jungle to rebounding echoic gunfire on mountains as key signifiers of sound whose origin, source, perspective, orientation, content and purpose are rendered invisible and hidden; disguised and undisclosed. Ducking and diving, the film directs one to experience an excess of the sonic with little or disparate visual correlation. True to its life-threatening and death-affirming din – and in total contradiction to the film's supposed veracity and all-bases-covered sound design – war in *Apocalypse Now* thus becomes the ultimate dislocation of sound from image.

Dir: Francis Ford Coppola; **Prod:** Francis Ford Coppola; **Scr:** John Milius, Francis Ford Coppola, Michael Herr; **DOP:** Vittorio Storaro; **Editor:** Lisa Fruchtman, Gerald B. Greenberg, Richard Marks, Walter Murch; **Score:** Carmine Coppola, Francis Ford Coppola; **Sourced Score:** Richard Wagner; **Sourced Songs:** The Doors, Jimi Hendrix; **Sound Design:** Walter Murch; **Main Cast:** Marlon Brando, Robert Duvall, Martin Sheen, Frederic Forest, Laurence Fishburne, Dennis Hopper.

Arashi ga oka (Onimaru)
Japan, 1988 – 143 mins
Yoshihige Yoshida

A meld of the seductive and the repulsive breathes through every audiovisual fibre that cross-threads *Arashi ga oka*, a spare Eastern-Gothic film loosely based on Emily Bronte's *Wuthering Heights*. Its atmospheric story is focused on the gradual psychological decay of Onimaru (Matsuda) after he disturbs a grave site. The film's cinematography consistently frames Onimaru and others in graceful contemplative pose, alienating their being in the spaces which trap them. Outdoors, minuscule figures carve elegant lines of movement across the barren spread of the Sacred Mountain (an unforgiving moonscape of volcanic grey). Indoors, the same figures are frozen in hermetic relief against the austere minimalism of the mountain's feudal mansions. Shifting between these two states of portraiture, an interlocked film score responds to the polarity of these settings.

Dynamically, the score enhances the many splits between emotional states and unleashed action; between repressed silence and uncontrolled utterance; between the vast ugly noise of the mountain and the strained beautiful ambience of the mansion. Whenever we are inside, we hear tuned wind draughts and tunnelled air vents; outside, we hear no natural sound effects, only the murmur of music and the rumble of ill-defined orchestration. Perceptively reverent of music's accord to film narrative, the score actively de-composes music as the situation warrants it, excusing itself of the heroic grandeur that typically accompanies high drama in Western cinema. The central thematic of decay – mortal, moral, mental – is clearly acknowledged in this approach.

With rooms that hum, wind that sings, walls that exhale and clothes that sigh, *Arashi ga oka* is a most potent musical example of how the Japanese soundtrack is the sound of the West turned inside out. This inversion is achieved not merely through established Japanese notions of *wabi-sabi* (the traditional aesthetic appreciation of flaws) and *ero-guro* (late 20s literary formulae combining sex and violence), but via a long-standing non-European legacy of what could be termed 'socio-acoustics'. Buildings, clothing, roads, food – all are formulated along entirely different materialist lines from those connected to Greek, Roman, Anglo-Saxon or Nordic traditions. Floors in Japanese houses are designed to be sounded, just as walls are designed to allow air through them; gardens are minds, water is time, silence is space. Things simply aren't what we in the West presume them to be. This means that our sense of Otherness works differently in an Oriental exploration of Otherness. It also means that how one designs sound for a room which allows outside sounds in, runs contrary to established design protocol. *Arashi ga oka* voices this through the heightened and mannered formation of its soundtrack.

When music is woven into this domestic fabric, the security blanket of Romantic musical conventions is rendered full of holes. While literary similarities can throw us life-savers and set up lighthouses for following its story, the musicalised atmospherics and sonar instrumentality of *Arashi ga oka* throw us deep into its aural mire of psychologically inferred space.

Dir: Yoshihige Yoshida; **Prod:** Kazunobu Yamaguchi; **Scr:** Yoshihige Yoshida; **DOP:** Junichiro Hayashi; **Editor:** Takao Shirae; **Score:** Toru Takemitsu; **Sound:** Sachio Kubota; **Main Cast:** Yusaku Matsuda, Yuko Tanaka, Rentaro Mikuni, Tatsuro Nadaka.

The Ballad of Narayama (*Narayama bushiko*)
Japan, 1958 – 98 mins
Keisuke Kinoshita

The Ballad of Narayama – centred on the crone Orin (Tanaka) as she is
about to retire to Mount Narayama and die now that she is seventy – is a
thoroughly cross-plotted, multi-voiced and double-checked transposition
of kabuki into cinematic form. The staging's artifice is glaringly apparent,
despite the comparatively 'natural' costuming of the characters. What is
less apparent is the way the camera's tracking shots constitute a mirrored
spatial articulation whose gesticulation meshes with the composed
movement of characters across the filmed stages. The camera is neither
documentary nor observational: it replicates stage direction similar to the
way scrims, backdrops and lighting actively 'compose space' directly in
front of one.

Yet *The Ballad of Narayama* is something more than merely a 'filmed
play': its cultural specificity severs it from how the stage – in theatre and
cinema – is defined in the West. The physicality of Western theatre is
most perverse when it stages an outdoor environment under the roof of
an auditorium. And the 'liveness' of theatre is rendered morbid when the
stage is composed not of fabricated designs, but of trees, flowers, dirt,
water, smoke: when players become strangely animated dolls, or humans
trapped in an over-sized diorama. The performative essence of theatre –
its forward thrust of the human body and its vocal projection into the
auditorium – never escapes the taxidermist's frame which posits and
artificialises players far more than the stilted and much-critiqued
proscenium arch. Whereas modern Western theatre is crisis-ridden by
this, Japanese kabuki honours it in a glorification of the human as doll,
mechanism, statue, outline. *The Ballad of Narayama*'s transposition of
kabuki into the photographic realm of cinema is thus angled away from
Western cinema's audiovisual forms.

The 'score' for *The Ballad of Narayama* is presented in unerring
replication of kabuki's multiple musical narration: the onstage *debayashi*

The Ballad of Narayama: an audiovisual transposition of kabuki into cinematic form

group of musicians, the raised *chobo* and the *joururi* singer who describes action, and the side-stage *geza* and its percussive accompaniment. These musical 'voices' take turns in modulating their description of the staged action, pausing at key points to allow an actor a line or two, and underscoring the many incidents of dramatic repression as actors withhold emotion in melodramatic pose. The pacing of description, narration and musical evocation superbly matches the movements of Orin as her ravaged body creeps from point A to B with a drawn-out intensity. Her final journey to the mountain on the back of her beloved son, Tatsuhei (Takahashi), takes on an epic scope, as the gravity of this being her last journey weighs heavily on Tatsuhei's mind.

The music's palpable grain – all *shimasen* scratches, *shakauhachi* squalls and *biwa* drones – foregrounds the energy of its performance, diluting its linguistic effect and heightening its sonic presence. Conversely, the near-total absence of atmospheres and sound effects creates an aural tomb for the proceedings, all of which occur in exterior or semi-exterior surrounds. And almost incongruously, music and dialogue are imbued with 'room' ambience. Yet just as walking on the floors of a traditional Japanese house sounds like you are walking on a raised wooden stage, actual and illusory sound merge without conflict on the kabuki stage. *The Ballad of Narayama* takes this further and completely redistributes live and dead audiovisual elements across the interlocking of its performative and staged platforms.

Dir: Keisuke Kinoshita; Prod: Masaharu Kokaji, Ryuzo Otani; Scr: Shichir Fukazawa, Keisuke Kinoshita; DOP: Hiroyuki Kusuda; Editor: Yoshi Sugihara; Score: Chuji Kinoshita; Songs: Matsunosuke Nozawa; Sound: Hisao Ono; Main Cast: Kinuyo Tanaka, Teiji Takahashi, Yuko Mochizuki.

Beneath the Valley of the Ultra-Vixens
US, 1979 – 93 mins
Russ Meyer

Despite this film's openly pornographic visuals, *Beneath the Valley of the Ultra-Vixens'* soundtrack ably competes with the film's hysterical imagery. Multiple narrators, talking dildos, orgasmic screams, collisions between muzak, radio, computer games and vinyl records all converge in a flagrant disregard for any semblance of audiovisual balance, narrative logic or symbolic sense.

The 'plot' – often deemed dismissable in pornography – has bearing on *Beneath the Valley of the Ultra-Vixens'* cinematic realisation. Lavonia (Natividad) throws out husband Rhett (Tracy) due to his desire to have anal sex with her. This leads him down a path of various aberrant exploits, while Lavonia embarks on ways to seduce him back to all options apart from anal. A variety of characters reveal the outrageous sexual grotesqueries of Small Town USA, each more bizarre and sexually confronting than the other. With its shaft firmly planted in pornography and only accidentally shooting itself into 'non-porn' cinema, *Beneath the Valley of the Ultra-Vixens* involves a 'reading' akin to trying out a sexual option to which one was hitherto blind. While outrageously camp on its surface (no one ever plays anything with a wink or a nod), the film is intent on making a mockery of those who presume the mainstream (as represented by Small Town USA) to be prudish, narrow and inexperienced. Yet it also rejects the expedient conventions of porn film-making and instead proffers narrative interference which fuses character with body in unusual ways.

The film's po-faced narration in the face of an array of utterly gravity-defying bodily types suggests that an alternative physics operates in this sexualised world. Forever turned-on, turned-up and sticking-out, bodily parts within and without *Beneath the Valley of the Ultra-Vixens* rule every frame and every second: continuity editing is discarded; nominal mix levels rejected; synchronism intensified. The film resembles more a hyper-cacophonic Warner Bros. cartoon staged on a Jacques Tati set, but behaving like a hard-core unleashing of libidinal energy into a Norman Rockwell centre-spread. The connections and relevance between sound and image are – in accordance with the film's fruity sexiness – liberated and liberating.

When The Very Big Blonde (Samples) plays Pong while wearing a revealing jump-suit (48–24–36), the electronic pings replicate the male-ogle shifting from bosom to bosom. Later, when she reaches ecstatic heights baptising Rhett live on her Baptist radio show after he has renounced anal sex, her screams send the VU meters peaking into the red again and again like a thrusting phallus. When Junkyard Sal (Mack) demands her employer Rhett satiate her mammoth sexual hunger, she jiggles her girth to the sound of cowbells and chains. By the film's defibrillated multiple endings (that come and come again in a rain of sexual confusion), Lavonia reverts to real-actress Kitten Natividad, whose sexual energy has grown to gargantuan proportions, leaving her to literally sit straddled atop California mountain peaks screaming 'More cock!' as her voice echoes across the undulating valleys of this audiovisual arcana of sexual Americana.

Dir: Russ Meyer; **Prod:** Russ Meyer; **Scr:** Roger Ebert, Russ Meyer; **DOP:** Russ Meyer; **Editor:** Russ Meyer; **Score:** William Tasker; **Sound Editor:** Russ Meyer; **Main Cast:** Stuart Lancaster, June Mack, Kitten Natividad, Steve Tracy, Pat Wright, Candy Samples.

The Birds
US, 1963 – 119 mins
Alfred Hitchcock

The opening credits to *The Birds* serve as an entry to the solely sonic domain of its soundtrack. As high-contrast visual abstractions of birds move across the frame, squeals and squawks attack the viewer's ears. A birdlike quality is felt, but these sounds are more alien than avian, more artificial than natural. Having been cued to read a mimetic representation of 'birds', we are jettisoned into experiencing a sensation of 'birdness'. This befits a story about birds whose behaviour defies ornithological precepts: these are not normal birds.

The credits distil a subjective impression of birds: you are not watching birds; you are being attacked by them. Soon, all modes of audiovisual depiction of actual birds and abstracted 'birdness' will exude dread as they carry the potential to be diametrically inverted. This is nothing short of a 'terror of illusion' – a specifically audiovisual illusion – central to *The Birds*' psychological horror.

There is much that is pregnant in *The Birds* due to a distribution of radical imbalances between the audio- and image-tracks. Highest degrees of this occur when music is absent, generating a specific 'sound of silence' which greatly enhances the film's peculiarly perverse dramatic tone. The birds themselves narratively thrive in non-musical silence. Rather than embodying or transmitting a superimposed musical logic which tags them as monstrous, malicious and maniacal, they speak in their own voice to their own kind. Their language is foreign, alien, avian, excluding us from the inner mechanisms of their motives and operations. In their manifold attacks, the birds orchestrate their own concrete cacophony.

Silence carries most dread in *The Birds*. Who or what is watching Melanie (Hedren) when she drives up to Bodago Bay in a string of undramatic wide shots? As in all voyeuristic vantage points, one experiences sight at the expense of sound. Melanie's drive is an archetypal cinematic reconstruction of this crucial aspect of the voyeuristic effect, one that here binds us, the film itself, and the birds. Only all three are capable of such telescoped viewpoints, and all three are perversely ensnared by *The Birds'* empty silence. This voyeuristic configuration peaks at the climactic gas station explosion, helplessly witnessed by Melanie, Mitch (Taylor) and other diner patrons. The scene's perspective shifts with the advent of the explosion, transporting us to a bird's-eye view. The microscopic melee below emits a thin trail of screams, lifted and dispersed by the hollow sound of upward-spiralling winds. Floating birds creep into the frame from all sides, gently hovering and letting loose occasional disinterested squawks.

After the deafening climax of one of many attacks on the household, Melanie cautiously checks the attic. All is still and quiet – until she unwittingly shines a torch on the massed birds roosted there like a cancer within the household. They swoop on her as she flails her arms desperately. Her cries for help slowly disintegrate into a field of whimpers, gasps and fluttering wings. The soundtrack impassively documents the deafening silence that ensues as her near-lifeless body is pecked by birds who now make no noise.

Dir: Alfred Hitchcock; Prod: Alfred Hitchcock; Scr: Evan Hunter; DOP: Robert Burks; Editor: George Tomasini; Score: Remi Gassman, Oskar Sala; Sound Recording: William Russell, Waldon O. Watson; Sound Consultant: Bernard Herrmann; Main Cast: Tippi Hedren, Rod Taylor, Jessica Tandy, Suzanne Pleshette, Veronica Cartwright.

Bitter Rice (*Riso amaro*)
Italy, 1950 – 107 mins
Giuseppi De Santis

Early in *Bitter Rice*, Sylvana (Mangano) says, 'I don't like to stay put'. An earthy sexual epigram, she characterises the transience which saturates neo-realist cinema: an obliterated landscape of urban/rural rubble, comprised of decentred outdoor locations where high noon seems forever fixed. People wander through these spaces with equal transience while sound and music waft in omnipresent whirls. Repeatedly in *Bitter Rice*, station announcements, trains chugging and women's choruses dissolve across successive spatial cuts, creating a series of sonic curves which never 'stay put'. Even the score – a grab-bag of fragmented piano tunes and halted timpani pulses – is more of a roving interloper to action than a rousing inspirer of emotion.

Bitter Rice opens with a radio announcer recording a documentary report on women rice-croppers. The film's camera apes the radio narrative and passes from the announcer to what he sees: a vast assemblage of refugee women workers boarding at a central train station. He introduces a worker who will tell listeners what it's like to perform her duties – but we never hear what she says. The camera drifts away like an itinerant to complete a 360-degree arc. Narrative, camera, space and voice are rendered transient, caught in the upheaval of economics which has created the huge influx of rice-croppers.

It is this influx that directs and controls *Bitter Rice* and to which the camera consistently returns. Abstracted yet formally beautified, the mass of women and their energy provide the fuel for the film's story. They are grouped as patterns which either replicate sonic waveforms and radiophonic diffusion, or wholly incorporate sound and music as manifestations of the women's energy. Forming concentric radiating lines like those of sound waves or water rings, the women perform tasks and rituals which symbolically tag the open-ended ways in which sound moves through the flat planes of neo-realist films. Pivotal to this sonar logic of circular orbs throughout *Bitter Rice* is Sylvana and her portable gramophone. Against rising hills and wearing rustic sandals, she dances on the dusty earth and broadcasts her sexual energy, attracting positive and negative forces in appreciation of her sono-sexual lure and creating an erotic centre for the barren shifting terrain around her.

One worker indoctrinates Sylvana to the sonar logic of the rice field: 'If you have anything to say, it's customary to sing it'. More so than spoken dialogue, clear ringing pitch shapes carry across space, proving that voice floats beyond divisions and broadcasts itself. Singing also motivates others to call-and-response, thereby energising social activity and even creating contests, as in the singing battle between the contract workers and the scabs. Even the opening of each irrigation gate is cued by a voice calling the name of the gate, creating a sonic score that maps the regulated flow of water that enriches the rice. This is extended to the film's tragic ending, when the women's collective emotional energy forms a visible shock wave as they encircle the body of Sylvana and remove their hats and cover her with handfuls of bitter rice.

Dir: Giuseppi De Santis; **Prod:** Dino De Laurentiis; **Scr:** Giuseppe De Santis, Carlo Lizzani, Franco Monicelli, Carlo Musso, Ivo Perilli, Gianni Puccini, Corrado Álvaro; **DOP:** Otello Martelli; **Editor:** Gabriele Varriale; **Score:** Goffredo Petrassi; **Songs:** Armandao Trovajoli; **Sound:** uncredited; **Main Cast:** Silvana Mangano, Maria Capuzzo, Doris Dowling, Vittorio Gassman.

Blade Runner
US, 1982 – 118 mins
Ridley Scott

The soundtrack to *Blade Runner* has been widely acknowledged for its contribution to both its ambience and the concept of 'ambience' in music. But this legacy does not derive from what is presumed to be its music alone. The blending of its synthesiser score with the film's atmospheres is responsible for the soundtrack's overall diffusion of faux-urban presences and pseudo-orchestral essences. The detailing and crafting of this aural interlacing understandably create the impression of a seamless soundscape whose musicality appears more atmospheric than composed, and whose sound design is orchestrated to perform in confluence with the score's feathered harmonic clouds which drift over a Los Angeles of the future. The topology of *Blade Runner* is largely celebrated as a sumptuous visual inventory of imaginary landscape, but its multi-layered soundtrack conveys the climatic conditions which shape the ambience of its world.

Key modernist traits are defined more by the film's mix of sonics and score. Amorphousness – sounds bleeding into and beyond the frame to suggest a non-specific space – and indifference – sono-musical lines being allowed to flow and resolve independent of focused dramatic occurrences – are noticeable in most of the breath-taking panoramas of the city. While these compositional techniques historically stem from the expanded notions of John Cage and Erik Satie respectively, their role in *Blade Runner* is rooted by a perversely futuristic narrative logic, informed by ideas of the collapsed metropolis and how time, space and people inhabit and navigate its reinvented zone. The composed score seemingly vaporises, as sounds from beyond its musically articulate realm reconfigure its authorial beam as a fluorescent bleeding of aural luminescence. This technique of stylistic diffusion in *Blade Runner* removes us from the pre-modern notion of the auditorium into its post-modern erasure and replacement by the 'acousmonium': a tactile, multi-directional and widely spaced presentation of sound.

Blade Runner's speculative Asianised LA generates a compounding of musical identities within a musicological matrix of impure forms and miscegenated styles: Japanese koto plucks, Greek bouzouki trills, Chinese wind chimes, Gregorian vocal drones, West African drumming, American jazz saxophones are all woven through the score. Acknowledging the seeping and saturating effect brought to bear on imperialist cultures as they are eventually transformed by colonised presences from within, *Blade Runner*'s ambience is a slightly disorienting but ultimately calming blend of multicultural discord and urban noise. LA's history is one of numerous cultural and anthropological seismic shifts; this futuristic projection is but one in a long chain. Essentially, *Blade Runner*'s LA is a horizontal diaspora reconfigured as a vertical metropolis, replacing cosmopolitan cultivation with cultural concentration, and expressing this transposition through musical multiplicity.

Blade Runner's mulatto musical modes as voiced by their synthetic and electronic simulations relate to the role of the replicants Rachel (Young), Pris (Daryl Hannah), Roy (Hauer) and others. Just as score and ambisonics are sprayed across a cinesonic canvas, and multifarious cultures are mixed into a social melting pot, the replicants' artificial creation and human conditioning are merged into a behavioural composite. In a world full of replicants, 'human' drama should not find comfortable roost. *Blade Runner* responds wisely to the psychological ramifications of its anti-egocentric narrative, and imperceptibly fuses music, sound and noise into a skin which could be you – or someone just like you.

Dir: Ridley Scott; **Prod:** Michael Deeley; **Scr:** Hampton Fancher, David Webb Peoples; **DOP:** Jordon Cronenweth; **Editor:** Terry Rawlings; **Score:** Vangelis; **Sound Editor:** Peter Pennell; **Sound Mix:** Budd Alper; **Main Cast:** Harrison Ford, Rutger Hauer, Sean Young, Edward James Olmos.

(Next page) Blade Runner: amorphousness and indifference in mixing sound and score

Blood Simple
US, 1983 – 97 mins
Joel Coen

Often perceived as an archly 'knowing' pastiche of film noir, *Blood Simple* is more a saturated audiovisual text than a clever game-play with cinephiles. Its meld of sound design and music score is testament to its materialist orientation: in a story where no one says what's on their mind, the soundtrack 'plays' the characters, taunting them in a deadly matrix of reflexivity and representation.

Blood Simple's complexity lies not in this play alone, but in the chameleon-like way the play shifts from traditional skilled crafting in its soundtrack to outwardly perverse staging of its cinesonic gestures. The logic in these shifts is only apparent on reflection: their momentary manifestation is swallowed up by envelopes of subterfuge and disinformation, pushing the film's narrative to play back on the viewer/auditor. From the opening title sequence and its abstracted orchestration of real and unreal sounds (thumping windscreen wipers over swelling subsonic rumbles), to its closing set-piece tensely predicated on multiple levels of characters engaged in a blind shoot-out with a wall between them, modes of knowing/telling and hearing/seeing dictate the film's construction and denouement.

Simple but aurally effective arrangement is evident in an early confrontation between Ray (Getz) and Marty (Hedaya). Tension is conjured from limited diegetic sounds: bar jukebox in the distance, deep rumbling of a background incinerator, incessant night crickets, a piercing insect-zapper. Rich in their presence, these sounds' volume levels and precise placement are determined by the scene's editing of dramatic performance. Gesturally reduced and stylised further is the sound of the ceiling fan in Marty's office. Functioning as an emotional metronome to his seething, brooding disposition, it throbs as an entirely unnaturalistic yet crucially fixed phoneme in the story. When Marty rings Abby but says nothing, she knows it's him because she knows his silent office ambience: its soft throb through the phone speaks of their estrangement from the other. When Marty is shot, the fan halts – then continues down tempo, signalling the psychoacoustic symbolism of the fan being Marty's dark heart beat.

Creating a webbing to the sound design's controlled orchestration is the score. Thematic assignment and economical exposition characterise the interlocking of *Blood Simple*'s musical cues, formulating a puzzle which describes the psychological links forged by the story's fatalistic love triangle. Early in the film, a key-frame melody is outlined by piano, playing over three concurrent scenes of Ray, Marty and Abby unable to sleep at night. The cue's rhythmic matrix responds to corresponding visual rhythms: Marty glaring at his ominous ceiling fan; Abby on a couch contemplating a smaller lounge room ceiling fan; Ray distracted by moving shadows cast upon the ceiling. A central tri-polar theme is musically narrated, detailing temporal and emotional relationships as the three characters wonder about themselves and the other two. The fixity with which their fates are entwined is encoded in the melodies: Marty is a low four-note ostinato gridlocked into repetition; Abby a high melody which flits with slight variations whose shape remains constant; Ray a note and its octave tick-tocking, unable to move forwards or backwards. This main theme returns in variations throughout the movie, reiterating the 'mélange' à trois spiralling suspicion.

Dir: Joel Coen; **Prod:** Ethan Coen; **Scr:** Ethan Coen, Joel Coen; **DOP:** Barry Sonnenfeld; **Editor:** Roderick Jaynes, Don Wiegmann; **Score:** Carter Burwell; **Sourced Song:** The Temptations; **Sound Editor:** Skip Lievsay, Michael R. Miller; **Special Sound Effects:** Fred Szymanski, Jun Mizumachi; **Main Cast:** John Getz, Frances McDormand, Dan Hedaya, M. Emmet Walsh.

Blue
UK, 1993 – 79 mins
Derek Jarman

A single-toned prayer bell rings to signal the start of *Blue*. So it commences; so it is sectioned; so it ends. A meditation on AIDS, the film exposes all it cannot show by refusing visuality and in place blinding one with its universe of blue; unmoving, unshifting, undiluted. *Blue* is a sonic poem whose image has been lost, whose visuality has been erased, and whose ocular sensuousness has faded with all that one remembers as the physicality of life and its acts of living.

'My retina is a distant planet' muses *Blue*'s multi-faceted unseen male voice. As he comes to terms with sightlessness, a narrative of planetary proportion grows from the scrims and scraps of his terminal diary. *Blue* is gorily poetic in its verbiage, its vividness coming equally from the bodily degradation it charts and the desire it holds for the caress of the living.

This is not to say *Blue* takes us nowhere and spirals downwards into a remorseful reflection of that which one can no longer enjoy. Rather, its absence of image intensifies the locations it imagines, describes, evokes. Detailing director Derek Jarman's descent into hospital treatments, mystical counselling and therapeutic consolation, the film is part elegiac autobiography and part snuff radio play. Its bitterness is not self-centred, but more a mourning for the loss of sight by a film-maker hitherto obsessed with poetic visuals of the most arch kind. *Blue*'s refusal of visuals stands as the director's most powerful and empowered statement, ironically as his vision fades while his mind remains alert and his body hyper-sensitive to the transformations he undergoes. A remarkable fixture to the present tense guides the film, grafting our aural imagination to the points and moments of his lack of sight: the sound of a woman from Edinburgh sobbing as the narrator himself is blinded by his own tears; an awareness of the hospital quiet as his sight closes in.

More bell rings: 'blue' becomes an ocean of the infinite; a vastness longed for beyond the purgatories which the AIDS patient bears like terrible stations of an inflicted cross. Time and again, the drudgery of hospitals is described with accompanying ambiences, rustling with muttering others and shuffling papers. This noise of the social, of its ant-like activity and bothersome scurrying, is posed as an irritant to the contemplative blueness to which the film's musical slivers and acoustic surfaces are attracted. Pockets of silence, pauses of room tone, after-rings of voices, fade-outs of whistling wind – all are cherished for their presence and their absence; all are aurally crafted as statements of their knowing disappearance, as one joins in the film's prayer 'to be released from image'.

Dir: Derek Jarman; **Prod:** James Mackay, Takashi Asai; **Scr:** Derek Jarman; **Score:** Simon Fisher-Turner; **Sound Design:** Marvin Black; **Voice Cast:** John Quentin, Nigel Terry, Derek Jarman, Tilda Swinton.

Blue Steel
US, 1990 – 103 mins
Kathryn Bigelow

In *Blue Steel*, Megan Turner (Curtis) is a rookie cop whose nervous strength and lithe stature sexually arouse the psychotically dispossessed Eugene Hunt (Silver) into stalking her. After failing to have him legally detained (because she had unwittingly invited him back to her apartment), Megan senses all public and personal space as a potentially threatening environment. Claustrophobia and agoraphobia collapse into a fear of space itself, as she finds familiar locales transformed into alien terrain. This is effectively cued throughout the movie by the subtle use of flanged wind (like one hears when breathing through a cardboard tube). Often, Megan will be framed at the end of a corridor in silhouette, light spilling in while we watch her from a distance. The combination of such overtly voyeuristic images with the tunnelling sound of air contributes to a 'phallic sound effect': an abstraction of the peeping Tom's breath, diffused into a penile stream of white noise which shoots towards Megan.

The title credits to *Blue Steel* establish this audiovisual symbolism clearly. Extreme close-ups track across and through the interlocking chambers, connected barrels and linked passages of a Smith & Wesson 38 Special. A scopic universe of metal if mapped, while sampled/looped breaths – sexual, mortal, fatal – breathe through this architecture formed of machine parts. The intricacies of gun design are enlarged to form a social macrocosm, charting both the urban entrapment of women and the psychological confines within which they must survive. The flanging-wind texture is amplified to convey the exhausted breath from both excited voyeur and fearful victim as predator encircles prey.

That wind texture connotes a contraction of space, evoking pipes, tubes and tunnels which are designed to irrigate flow under heightened

(Opposite page) Blue Steel: phallic sound effects and aural cum shots

pressure, as liquid or air will pass more quickly and with greater force down a narrow canal than a wide thoroughfare. The notion of 'phallic' characteristics here is not to do with mere visual similarities in vertical form (a gross misunderstanding of penile mechanics within the body construct), but more to do with the control of energy and its transformation into the securing of power. Just as a woman's scream in modern cinema is an aural cum shot – externalised, airborne, explosive – the hollow sound of tunnelled air is an aural hard-on: internalised, fluid-driven, raging. *Blue Steel* focuses on the build-up more than the climax; on the urges and impulses which heave and sigh within the male corpus more than the screams unleashed from the victimised female. Megan is not another Pauline tied to perilous railway tracks; nor is she facilely spooked and shocked by unexpected attacks from her assailant. She is gradually granted an overview – a schematic map – of her stalker's methods, machinations, miasma and mania. From that vantage point, she can audibly discern his panting breath from her own nervous gasps; she can locate him, fix him, frame him, freeze him (as occurs in the final shoot-out in an emptied downtown street). Far from being silenced, Megan silences herself. Empowered through knowing the sound of his voice, she refrains from giving him that which he most desires: her scream.

Dir: Kathryn Bigelow; **Prod:** Edward R. Pressman, Oliver Stone; **Scr:** Kathryn Bigelow, Eric Red; **DOP:** Amir M. Mokri; **Editor:** Lee Percy; **Score:** Brad Fiedel; **Supervising Sound Editor:** Richard King; **Main Cast:** Jamie Lee Curtis, Ron Silver, Clancy Brown.

Boogie Nights
US, 1997 – 155 mins
Paul Thomas Anderson

Boogie Nights sets the agenda for how songs can be used to culturally locate a story, rather than perfunctorily slot them into a radiophonic histogram. While the film charts the chaotic state of the porn industry at the end of the 70s, the music peels back the scab of collective forgetfulness to prod the fetid sono-semiotics of songs like Apollo 100's 'Joy', Nena's '99 Luft Balloons' and Electric Light Orchestra's 'It's a Miracle'. But not a smidgen of camp is to be found, so forget such terms when journeying through the wood-grained multi-track mixing consoles which blanket the texture of the film's soundtrack with the gorgeous slump of late-70s/early-80s pop/rock.

Boogie Nights deftly employs songs like aural production design, matching antique synths to gaudy wallpaper, Ibanez fuzz-wahs to the lighting in convenience stores, and compressed snare thuds to ritzy cowboy boots. Most fascinating – and the modus operandi behind the film's weaving of genuine emotional warmth amid its decidedly retro iconography – is the film's placement of songs in mismatched settings. This is usually achieved by starting a song in one scene and then allowing it time and space to flow into the next scene. The resultant effect imbues the song with a disturbing ambivalence that simultaneously drains the song of an 'event' status and displaces it into the amorphous backgrounding of the film's psychological ambience. Songs, then, perform as cues, and are less edited (which is nominally a process of turning the song on or off in a film) and more orchestrated so as to conduct the characters' emotional energies.

Beyond mere coincidence or pointed synchronicity, many characters are staged in the act of consuming music. In some cases this technique is used to deepen a character's make-up (prompted by Jack Horner – Reynolds – himself playing 'The Sage' after a hard day's porno-making). In some cases, song nurtures empathy (pinpointed by Buck Swope –

Cheadle – desperately affecting alignment with bass in C&W and gel in Rick James). And in others, song sharpens their psychosis (exhibited by Rahad Jackson – Alfred Molina – notching up his coke-addled energy to an epiphanous moment in 'Jessie's Girl'). Ultimately, *Boogie Nights* is unironic, and not to be confused with lesser cinematic flings with pop music. This is unavoidably noticeable during the intercutting of Dirk (Wahlberg) and Roller Girl's (Graham) lowest moments as the sound of a slowed-down record player – complete with crackles – plays a dark lumbering pattern. The bleakness of the late night Sherman Oaks wasteland which traps them is transformed into a black cave of sound, opened by the music's inner groove, signifying dread, danger and dire consequences. (This dark throb thins out into background radio playing 'Silent Night' when Buck is trapped in the middle of a messy convenience store hold-up: the preceding scene's sonic darkness actually sounds like 'Silent Night' played on a malfunctioning record player.)

Boogie Nights works beyond one's ontological schema of cinema; it works in the dense fibrous sonorum of pop music, record production, and the strikingly ambivalent evocation specific to lyric writing. More than a film that 'uses' song, it is a film that knows song – its flirtatious socio-cultural pomp and circumstance. In doing so, *Boogie Nights* reaches a height of 'vertical narration', where everything is told – as songs do – 'all at once'. Bypassing literary models, this film is a timbrel text which must be listened to in order for it to be read.

Dir: Paul Thomas Anderson; Prod: Paul Thomas Anderson, Lloyd Levin, John Lyons, Joanne Sellar; Scr: Paul Thomas Anderson; DOP: Robert Elswit; Editor: Dylan Tichenor; Score: Michael Penn; Sourced Score: Jon Brion; Sourced Songs: include Emotions, Boney M, Chico Hamilton Quartet, the Chakachas, Three Dog Night, Eric Burdon and The Animals, Elvin Bishop, Starland Vocal Band, Apollo 100, Melanie, Juice Newton, The Commodores, Hot Chocolate, Sniff and the Tears, Rick Springfield, Nena, the Beach Boys, Electric Light Orchestra; Supervising Sound Editor: Dane A. Davis; Main Cast: Mark Wahlberg, Burt Reynolds, Julianne Moore, Don Cheadle, Philip Baker Hall, Philip Seymour Hoffman, William H. Macy, John C. Reilly, Heather Graham.

California Split
US, 1974 – 108 mins
Robert Altman

A rarity in the majorly artificial realm which governs film soundtrack production, *California Split* contains no non-diegetic or extra-diegetic sound. All sounds occurring on the film's soundtrack emanate from an acoustic spatial location within the film. While this adoption of documentary technique promotes aural realism, its application here is guided by dramatic purpose.

The characters of Charlie Waters (Gould) and William Denny (Segal) are pivotal to the film's undulating soundscape. Garrulous and continually cutting into and talking over one another, their voices are more oral performance than scripted dialogue. Recorded with radio microphones, they rove and roam the noisy din of gambling establishments, improvising ceaselessly and breathlessly. There they interact with a mix of actors and non-actors. The latter's hesitant, fluctuating and mumbled delivery conveys a richness that could not be acoustically recreated or theatrically simulated. Furthermore, the soundtrack does not privilege Charlie and William above others. The sound of a babbling bartender will be just as loud as Charlie when he is delivering an important piece of dialogue; injections by an off-screen extra will dogfight with William's banter.

Noise (as a multiple of sound levels) and silence (as either an absence, an isolation or a softening of those sounds) work to distinguish *California Split*'s plot flows and character development. When there is an excess of sound (the horse track, card games and poker halls) the narrative conveys a continuum of character action. When there is noticeable silence (as in William's many reflective moments) the narrative signals a change in character orientation. Reflecting the psychological ramifications of accumulated sound in social spaces, noise (of both their surroundings and their own babbling) keeps Charlie and William from breaking their compulsion to gamble;

sudden silences initiate a pause wherein they can reflect and make a decision to change their situation.

While there appears to be music in *California Split* (those raspy boogie piano songs), it only temporarily functions as non-diegetic sound. Two striking aspects determine this. Firstly, the songs sound 'live', eschewing the clinical silence expected of studio recording. The piano recordings contain much background noise, plus they have a loose and unstructured feel about them. Secondly, we eventually see the location of these songs: the piano player in Reno (Phyllis Shotwell).

However, this is not to say that the songs are merely live on-location recordings. Our 'visual discovery' of the hitherto invisible songs' source and location centralises Reno within the narrative. Reno is where Charlie and William reach a peak and then depart to go their separate ways. Reno is the zenith of their transient relationship with one another. As the credits roll to Charlie's last spin of a roulette wheel, *California Split* reunites on-screen sound with on-screen image as closure to the film's emotional dislocation-stretched synchronism.

Dir: Robert Altman; **Prod:** Robert Altman, Leonard Goldberg, Aaron Spelling, Joseph Walsh; Scr: Joseph Walsh; **DOP:** Paul Lohmann; **Editor:** Lou Lombardo; **Songs Performed By:** Phyllis Shotwell; **Sound Mix:** James E. Webb; **Sound Editor:** Kay Rose; **Main Cast:** George Segal, Elliot Gould.

Carnival of Souls
US, 1962 – 83 mins
Herk Harvey

A woman – bruised, tattered, covered in mud – emerges from a river's edge where earlier her car had been retrieved after she was driven over the bridge into murky waters. Dredging fails to recover the car, but now Mary (Hillgoss) mysteriously returns in a daze, unable to communicate clearly. She gives rise to strange visceral combinations: moist and muddy, sweaty and sexual, ravaged and rebirthed, traumatised and terrifying, erotic and ectoplasmic. This is the body of the cinematic scream held in *Carnival of Souls*: a catatonic corpus whose silence articulates all that is connoted by the tightly phased collision of cinematic screams with social screams.

Carnival of Souls is mostly post-dubbed and echoes many a 60s 'adult movie' with its flat vocalisation as Mary drifts through the scenes in a strangely detached manner. But simpatico with the film's haunting story, Mary is in fact dead. And as she ethereally floats in the mortal world of tangible substances, so her quivering on the film soundtrack separates her from on-screen presence. Yet Mary does not realise she is dead. The 'souls' of the dead follow to reclaim her and return her to the domain of the departed, leading her to believe she is being chased by a strange man visible only to her.

After Mary tries on a dress in a department store change room, she returns to the sales clerk, who now can neither see nor hear her. Mary thinks she is being ignored but then becomes aware – as we do – of the profound silence which embalms her presence. The soundtrack is totally devoid of all atmosphere and ambience – what studio engineers refer to as an acoustically 'dead' space. If Mary only knew of this sonic morbidity, she would realise her unalterable predicament. Unfortunately prompted by the privilege of sight in the mortal world, she believes that which appears before her eyes, when her hearing alone grants absolute truth.

Carnival of Souls: breath on the soundtrack is erotic and necrotic

This unsettling audiovisual effect recalls similarly alienating moments in our actual acoustic existence: the blocking of the ear due to changes in atmospheric pressure in a plane cabin; the lodging of water in the ear canal after a swim; watching people on the street through sealed doubled-glazed glass windows without hearing their speech. These commonplace situations wrench sound from sight, upsetting the balance struck in stable sono-optical conditions. In place, we clearly audit our own internal breathing but register only the slightest and radically diminished occurrence of all external action we witness. Our very breath – the most tangible trace of our mortality – haunts us.

Mirroring the frightening ambiguousness of the female scream, breath on the soundtrack is both erotic and necrotic. It replaces the presence of the actor and his/her character with a bodily occupation of audiovisual space. The screen and its acoustic field become a terrain no longer inhabited by silvery ghosts, but by a corporeal funk of glottal spittle and nasal whistle. When Mary realises that no one can see or hear her, she becomes aware of her bodily status as a shell traversing a world in which she is not welcome, leaving her to roam mismatched, desynchronised, acoustically alienated.

Dir: Herk Harvey; **Prod:** Herk Harvey; **Scr:** John Clifford; **DOP:** Maurice Prather; **Editor:** Dan Palmquist, Bill de Jarnette; **Score:** Gene Moore; **Sound:** Ed Down, Don Jessup; **Main Cast:** Candace Hilligoss, Sidney Berger.

Car Wash
US, 1976 – 97 mins
Michael Schultz

It is strange how 'film music' so often bears ungainly traces of its origins from the wrong side of the screen. Originally bellowing and trumpeting itself from the aptly named 'orchestra pit', film music paid its dues looking up at the screen's stellar sheen, yearning for that glory. Come its marriage to image on the soundtrack – a technological nuptial of sorts – its neurotic insecurity did not dissipate. Stuck in a limelight that privileges the visual and the optical as people 'watch' movies but rarely listen to them, film music continues with its attention-grabbing measures, compensating for its invisibility with desperate non-diegetic direction.

Car Wash is comfortable with its music not being part of the screen. It loosens up and relaxes its sense of place in relation to the screen, and generates a more dynamic musical statement. Responding to the communal production and local reception of music which propels many streams of funk, soul and disco, it imports an entirely different sense of musical location into the cinema. The film's story develops from a motley bunch working at a car wash in Los Angeles. With the employees being predominantly African American (including a Jewish kid who dreams of 'being black'), the radio played on the PA system is tuned to a funky station which plays the song score to the film. Following the blaxploitation strategy of commissioning known musical composers/producers/arrangers to supply song scores, *Car Wash*'s music is as stylistically integrated as its African-American community of workers is segregated into a social microcosm of the car wash.

Music thus does not arise from 'somewhere else' in *Car Wash*: it comes from within its group and circulates within its cultural terrain. It is not there to 'represent' people or races; rather, it is indivisible from them. This direct attachment and inseparability of music, character, lifestyle, market and type greatly reduce any distance between sound and image, and between narrative and song. Not surprisingly, the employment of songs by 'non-film-music-composers' has been traditionally frowned upon and dismissed. This is unfortunate, because a film like *Car Wash* deliberately mines its musicological depth to refine its social critique.

While American radio had by the 70s become synonymous with mobility of listening and a fracturing of music markets, *Car Wash* centres radio as a fixed focal point around which its characters circulate. From moments of collective celebration as the crew boogies to the film's theme song in escapist joy despite the somewhat mechanised tasks they undertake, to the desperate dreams of T.C. (Ajaye) as he tries to win a phone-in contest so he can impress the beautiful but haughty Marsha (Melanie Mayron), to the politicised disgust Abdullah (Duke) shows for his co-workers grooving while working for the man, *Car Wash* uses its radiophonic score broadcast as a backdrop against which its characters are presented. Effectively, this would be not unlike the musicians from the 'pit' jumping up on stage and mixing it with the actors. Desirous of 'dancing in the streets with music everywhere', *Car Wash* imports its deliriously funky score not from a dismissive lowly state, but from the social and communal ambience which energises the air of any collective gathering.

Dir: Michael Schultz; **Prod:** Art Linson, Gary Stromberg; **Scr:** Joel Schumacher; **DOP:** Frank Stanley; **Editor:** Christopher Holmes; **Song Score:** Norman Whitfield, Rose Royce; **Sound Editor:** Peter Berkos, Roger Sword; **Main Cast:** Franklyn Ajaye, Bill Duke, Antonio Fargas.

Cast Away
US, 2000 – 143 mins
Robert Zemeckis

Cast Away is less about the stranding of Chuck Noland (Hanks) on an uncharted island, and more about the insertion of a living human into an inanimate freight system. Noland's reconstitution as freight is forecast early in the film, as a package is shuttled from the middle of America to the centre of Russia. The feeling of 'being freight' is heightened as we are lost in a dark jungle of illegible dialogue, muted atmospheres, murky light, askew angles. Two distinct audiovisual 'movements' prior to the landing of Noland on the island develop his freight state. Firstly, during the plane trip: the drone of the aeroplane engines creates a vibrating dynamo of still energy, which induces a psychoacoustic folding of claustrophobia with inertia. Immobile and taciturn as we tend towards when travelling by plane, Noland is less a passenger and more a package. Secondly, after the plane has crashed into the ocean: a series of blackouts appear between sporadic flashes of lightning while the ocean roars unremittingly, tragically marking a line of dots on a map that no one will find. Noland becomes a message in a bottle on a dead sea, not so much by floating into the unknown as by 'becoming the undelivered': no one will be hearing from him for some time.

Once on the island, Noland has to realign his audiovisual balance. Terrorised by the sound of the unknown, he hears 'bumps in the night', which prove to be strange fruit falling from trees. No living being directed these events; just the life of the island, devoid of such controlled presence. Eventually, Noland gets to read the island as a manual of patterns, frequencies and ratios: from the seasonal changes in wind directions, to the movement of fish underwater, to the many environmental sounds that define the terrain of the island.

Music appears a whole hour into the film as Noland leaves the island on his makeshift raft. The prior absence of music perfectly reflects the dehumanising of Noland's status as freight by refuting humanist commentary on his apparent hopelessness. Notably, music enters only when hope takes hold within his psyche. As he passes the barrier of rocks, he is inserted back into the passage of freight along which the FedEx plane journeyed. Rooted on the island, he was a dead letter; caught in the flow of the sea, he is once again in circulation. Here the camera evidences the space beyond the site of his plight, and in doing so liberates us from the sound of sand, the reverb of rocks, and the timbre of timber which had built a sonorum for his island entrapment.

Over the end credits, the refrain of music which hardly marked the film sails forth. But then a quiet mystical gesture is struck which confirms the considered modulation of humanism of *Cast Away*: the sound of waves gradually fades up and builds in mass, eventually dissolving the score. Music thus becomes the ocean – an ebb and flow of tidal call-and-response to itself; the ocean thus becomes air – the totality of atmosphere which carries sound.

Dir: Robert Zemeckis; **Prod:** Tom Hanks, Jack Rapke, Steve Starkey, Robert Zemeckis; **Scr:** William Boyles Jr; **DOP:** Don Burgess; **Editor:** Arthur Schmidt; **Score:** Alan Silvestri; **Sound Design:** Randy Thom; **Main Cast:** Tom Hanks, Helen Hunt.

Citizen Kane
US, 1941 – 119 mins
Orson Welles

If *Citizen Kane* is figuratively and literally about one's last word –
Charles Kane's (Welles) enigmatic utterance of 'Rosebud' – it is also
about the 'preverberation' and reverberation which hold that utterance
centre stage in the film's auditorium. Furthermore, *Citizen Kane* is not
a priori a visual film: it is a sonic, acoustic, vocal text. Its beams of
light, shafts of luminance, patterns of shadow are *post partum*
visualisations of vocal presences, melodic flows, sonorous atmospheres.
True to the mystery which propels the story, there is much that is not
spoken in *Citizen Kane*. Yet most of what isn't said is textually voiced
through the human voice – through its presence, power, musicality and
breath.

Citizen Kane's casting of actors acknowledges their vocal timbre,
phrasing, and pitch modulation. Ensemble interactions exude a
thrilling sense of audible orchestration as they weave in and out of
each other, just as each solo performance carries variance in delivery
and dynamic range. Having such clearly delineated vocal identities,
Citizen Kane deftly combines their lines of delivery through both
deceptive and forthright shifts in volume levels. Rather than simply
employing overlapping dialogue, the film consistently modulates the
volume of every character's voice to further shape the dramatic
material.

We first hear the youthful Kane's voice as he turns in his office chair
to face Mr Carter (Erskine Sanford). Kane eloquently, snidely and
confidently returns each exasperated retort of Carter's in a virtuoso
display of verbal volleys: this man could talk anyone into anything; his
power is in his voice. An image of Kane develops that wavers between
passionate dedication to a cause and manic obsession with control. The
more he exerts falsehood, the more he bluffs and the more
commandeering his voice (as in his grandstanding rally speech). But

Citizen Kane: a *post partum* visualisation of vocal presence

when he is truthful, he is quiet, withdrawn, modest (as when he reads his declaration of principles).

Kane's first impression of Susan Alexander (Comingore) is of her voice: he stands splattered with mud while she giggles uncontrollably at his misfortune. He berates her and hears her speak through a tensed jaw due to her toothache. Moving to her boudoir, she sings for him accompanying herself at the piano. In her quiet domestic space, her voice charms Kane, soothing his fixation on worldly issues with her disarming naiveté and quaint personality. Unfortunately for Susan, Kane is enthralled by the effect she has upon him; he will soon be intaking her voice like a drug.

Just as we can uncover the complex audiovisual mechanisms which drive *Citizen Kane*'s formal construction by listening to it, so too can we fully perceive the dynamics of Kane's psyche by listening to the effect it has on the voice of Susan Alexander. She is the sonic key, the aural lock and the vocal gateway to the pressure that builds up on Kane for him to explode, expire and enunciate 'Rosebud'.

Dir: Orson Welles; **Prod:** Orson Welles; **Scr:** Orson Welles; **DOP:** Gregg Tolland; **Editor:** Robert Wise; **Score:** Bernard Herrmann; **Sourced Score:** Richard Wagner, Giocchino Rossini, Frederic Chopin; **Sound:** John Aalberg; **Special Sound Effects:** Harry Essman; **Main Cast:** Orson Welles, Joseph Cotton, Dorothy Comingore, Agnes Moorhead, Ray Collins, Everett Sloane, Ruth Warrick.

A Clockwork Orange
UK, 1971 – 137 mins
Stanley Kubrick

Liberal cinema tends to subscribe to the notion that society is to blame for most ills. Championed as an investigation of the social forces which can control the individual, *A Clockwork Orange* in fact proposes the opposite. The 'problem' is not the world; clearly, it is Alex (McDowell). The score points the finger loudly.

Alex stomps across a landscape stamped with sociologically scarring potential, yet his external environment is not alien, other, or threatening. The problem is in his head. In there, the 2nd movement of Beethoven's 9th Symphony rings and climaxes until overcome by something else – a rich, swirling metallic tone, tuned to the tonic of the piece and evoking a huge bell. As depicted when Alex is trapped in a room above giant speakers blasting Beethoven up through the floorboards, this is pure sonic terror: a ringing sound you can't get out of your head that keeps you awake all night. In this case, it is the tonal underbed to an electronic rendition of Beethoven's 9th. This electronic realisation of Beethoven conveys the subjective perspective of someone listening to Beethoven and, moreover, being driven by the music. The synthesiser is being employed not simply to create imagined worlds and evoke mental states, but to de-interiorise the mind of a character: to turn that character's inner world inside out by creating a musical soundscape which we as viewer/auditors inhabit. A wholly cinesonic post-theatre effect, the strains of Beethoven in *A Clockwork Orange* do not beckon Alex like a snake charmer's clarinet; they are the sinuous, treacly threads of his own problematised psychological make-up.

The electronic score to *A Clockwork Orange* is an unacknowledged figure in the musicological development of the synthesiser. In its queasily affective sonic palette, those chintzy analogue tones embodying centuries-old melodies are historically implausible yet technologically possible. Simplistic linear thought labels this 'new-meets-old' but the implications are lateral. The score plays Beethoven as 'heard' by a synthesiser, and thereby – devoid of irony – demonstrates the synthesiser's unique ability not simply to 'represent' something, but to take its place. The synthesised renderings of Beethoven, Rossini and Elgar in *A Clockwork Orange* execute those composers' pieces via sonic textures which obliterate the very work being performed. Once you introduce such a severely self-reflexive and radically dimensional effect into the already overloaded receptive domain of the cinematic experience, 'reading' the film becomes a complex affair.

Synthesisers as used in a film like *A Clockwork Orange* become crucial instruments in expanding modern and post-modern aspects of film as an audiovisual medium. The greater depths of *A Clockwork Orange* are to be found in the many ways that its self-deconstructed score undercuts the sociological programme of its morals and themes. Alex works his way through a complete cycle: being aberrant, admonished, convicted, rehabilitated, and finally readmitted to his own psychic ward of sexualised violence. The music in his head, though, remains other than itself, granting him a disturbing stability in his own psychosis.

Dir: Stanley Kubrick; **Prod:** Stanley Kubrick; **Script:** Stanley Kubrick; **DOP:** John Alcott; **Editor:** Bill Butler; **Score:** Wendy Carlos; **Sourced Score:** Ludwig van Beethoven, Gioacchino Rossini, Edward Elgar; **Sourced Song:** Nacio Herb Brown; **Sound:** Brian Blamey; **Main Cast:** Malcom McDowell, Patrick Magee, Aubrey Morris, Warren Clarke, Sheila Raynor, Philip Stone.

Close Encounters of the Third Kind (Special Edition)
US, 1977 – 132 mins
Steven Spielberg

While sci-fi has traditionally created novel images, forms and terrain whose weirdness signifies the non-human, *Close Encounters of the Third Kind* fixates on the banal domesticity of human life (of the American kind). Visually and mythically, this veneer has been associated with an overbearing humanism, yet a purpose in its suburban/rural idyllicism is revealed when one considers how sound and music relate to this humanist domain.

Close Encounters poses alien life form not as aberrant interference, but as communicable presence: the reason for the aliens' visitation is to dialogue and exchange. Their attempts in this area move through a series of phenomenological transgressions which do not obey the laws of earth's physics. Gravity, mass, electricity, light and sound are all turned helter-skelter when spaceships come into contact with humans. All that was previously inanimate or dormant in the film's exhaustively documented 'homescapes' becomes activated and energised by the aliens' proximity to the human field. Humans are similarly affected: Roy (Dreyfuss), Jillian (Dillon) and many others not only bear radiation tan, but their minds have been impregnated with subliminal data: the image of Devil's Tower in Wyoming where the mothership will land, plus the building blocks to the aliens' language in the form of a musical motif (D, E, C, C, G – a cunning mutation of Roy's baby-boomer identification with 'When You Wish Upon a Star').

While a purposely chosen cross section of plainfolk men, women and children are impelled to meet the aliens, learned analysts headed by Lacombe (Truffaut) read the signs of alien presence from an external perspective. They have not enjoyed any internalised dialogue, so they are left to consider everything as linguistic intervention rather than transcendental correspondence. From patterned blips on shortwave to massed Indians chanting the musical motif, the refrain becomes a sacred sonic tablet whose numerical ratio of mathematical frequencies contains a key for replying to the aliens. Throughout many scenes of suspense as aliens make initial contact and humans strive to comprehend their mission, the score extols a superb hesitancy in forming tonal progression. Single notes, swelling fixed chords, shimmering overtones and slow timbrel glissandos collectively map points of contact as humans and aliens converge. Only when familiarity and comfort are established does the score form more recognisable parts.

When the mothership finally lands, music disappears entirely as a set of tuned subsonic rumbles match the ship's stultifying mass. In the silence that follows, a technician tentatively plays the musical motif on a gigantic organ, responding to a barrage of numerical and analytical instructions by assembled musical analysts, physicists and linguists. Like the architects of Babel, they anxiously compose in front of the levitated monolith; it plays back the refrain and blasts out the glass window of a tower. Soon, a dialogue of sorts is established, which – despite confusing both parties – sets them both at ease. 'Everyman'-Roy gets to enter that star of his dreams, and inside the mothership – more a giant mall than a vessel interior – the score transforms into choral arrangements. Human/alien union ultimately occurs through the close encounter resulting from aliens mirroring sonic human language: music.

Dir: Steven Spielberg; **Prod:** Julia Phillips, Michael Phillips; **Scr:** Steven Spielberg; **DOPs:** William A. Fraker, Douglas Slocombe, Vilmos Zsigmond; **Editor:** Michael Kahn; **Score:** John Williams; **Supervising Sound Effects Editor:** Frank E. Warner; **Main Cast:** Richard Dreyfuss, François Truffaut, Terri Garr, Melinda Dillon, Bob Balaban.

Colors
US, 1987 – 126 mins
Dennis Hopper

The opening title to *Colors* is superimposed over shots of East LA seen through the window of a roaming cop car. A spray can 'bloods' the screen with red title lettering; it's aural presence sounds like it has been smeared onto the cinema screen itself. From this point on, the cinema space is configured as a threatening zone, a territorial realm where you as an audience member are under threat. Constantly and consistently, sounds come from behind, above, extreme left and right so that one is always left suspecting there is more than what is depicted on the screen. As such, off-screen sounds of screams, gunshots, sirens, footsteps, breaths are signs of potential death in the black night of the urban jungle. Before too long one is engaged in 'reading' sounds as cues for survival. The deep hum of cruising low-riders nearing their drive-by, the fractured electro and Latin hip-hop beats from a boom-box, the yelping of killer dogs chained to the wire mesh of desolate front yards – all are signs of one gang transgressing the turf of another, and clarion calls for inevitable clashes and violence. This is all handled by sonic means, accentuating the sonar nature of urban gang warfare and transporting it onto the film's soundtrack.

The placement of gunshots in *Colors*' mix is designed to psychoacoustically convey the effect of being shot, using high-pitched clicks to peak percussive impact and diffused low thuds to rack the body with queasiness. The gunshots' spread of frequencies in the surround space is crucial to the sound enveloping you, just as it is intended that you do not simply observe human tragedy but you sense it through noting your own irrationally emotional reaction to being manipulated in this way. Taking its cue from the incessant use of gunshot sound effects in hip hop over the preceding decade and a half, *Colors* replays the fetishisation of those sounds and intensifies them. To tone them down would amount to a denial of the social reality of vicious crime circles within which so much of black America is trapped.

Colors: occupying the auditorium through sonic extremism

But even if one chooses to dismiss the death aesthetic the film relishes, it is hard to ignore the film's predominance of bass. *Colors* is a film that lets bass boom vociferously in the auditorium. The title track by Ice-T is mixed into the film soundtrack without diluting the power of its 808 kick, making the music take on the full sensory throb of a club environment. Bass is acceptable in film sound as earthquakes, spaceships and the voice of God – but the sheer electronic intensity of drum machines and sampled loops usually finds but mere crevices for placement in the final mix of a film. *Colors* uses its subsonic musical pulsation to reframe the frequency range one expects of music cue placement on the soundtrack. Exploiting the wilful and heady excessiveness that energises music that is 'too black – too strong', *Colors* occupies the cinema auditorium through sonic extremism, and celebrates the earthy totality of hip hop's aural landscape.

Dir: Dennis Hopper; **Prod:** Robert H. Solo; **Scr:** Robert Di Lello, Michael Schiffer; **DOP:** Haskell Wexler; **Editor:** Robert Estrin; **Score:** Herbie Hancock; **Songs:** Ice-T, Decadent Dub Team, Salt-N-Pepa, Big Daddy Kane, Eric B. and Rakim, Kool G. Rap, 7A3, Roxanne Shante, M.C. Shan, Rick James; **Sound Design:** Gary Rydstrom, Randy Thom; **Main Cast:** Sean Penn, Robert Duvall, Maria Conchita Alonso, Don Cheadle.

The Colour of Paradise (*Rang-e khoda*)
Iran, 1999 – 90 mins
Majid Majidi

The Colour of Paradise might seem an obvious title to describe the trials and tribulations of a young blind boy, Mohammad (Ramezani), whose cold-hearted father attempts to disown him by various means. Certainly a bleakness wraps itself around this heart-wrenching tale of child exploitation to which global art-house cinema is most attracted. However, rounded control of the film's intersticed image- and soundtracks shifts the film from simply wearing its heart on its sleeve to amplifying its eyes and projecting its ears.

The film opens with the final day of class at a school for the blind. Slabs of cassette audio are diced and sliced as a teacher plays fragments, asking each time whose cassette he is playing. Unseen voices excitedly respond. Another teacher slowly reads a poem as the children transcribe it in Braille, her sonorous voice bathed in a sea of clattered paper-punching. The children read back what they have written; their hands soft and tender, just like their whispered voices.

Alone in the dormitory after his father has not come to retrieve him, Mohammad listens to a cassette of an echoic voice singing longingly for another Mohammad. His loneliness is exaggerated by his knowing that she sings for someone else. Yet once he returns outside to continue his wait, the chirping of a bird snares his attention. Sonically attuned, he reads it as a baby bird fallen from a nest. A cat's snarl alerts him to imminent danger; he hurls rocks at the cat and hones in on the bird's chirps like a saviour bat. Though Mohammad is seemingly abandoned by his own father, his sense of responsibility to the world is achingly portrayed. When Mohammad's father (Mahjoub) finally appears, he spies on Mohammad from afar, almost disgusted by the sight of his blind son. Our witnessing of the father's inhuman behaviour and harsh impassivity casts our relation to Mohammad's blindness under compromising terms from this point on: fear is instilled for the familial livelihood of this lost child.

Mohammad is oblivious to this due to his innate humanitarianism more than his mere blindness, and his innocence is highlighted by his hyper-tactile relation to the world around him. He listens to birds and insects with undying amazement; he grasps the wind and massages the surface of water as if they are gold; he smells fragrances like they are gifts from the heavens. While the film's cinematography is controlled and unmannered, its sound design quivers in response to Mohammad's waves of aural consciousness. His aura is affective and magical. As he calls across the rolling hills to his grandmother Aziz when approaching the family farm, his voice enlivens the space. His sisters hear him: their faces beam knowing that Mohammad has returned.

The Colour of Paradise uncompromisingly charts the tragic path Mohammad is forced to take, but not once does it resort to maudlin musical commentary, over-privileged performances by its cast, or stilted cinematographic metaphor. For the colour of paradise which is Mohammad's unerringly positive world is all the wonderful sound around him.

Dir: Majid Majidi; **Prod:** Mehdi Karimi; **Scr:** Majid Majidi; **DOP:** Hashem Attar, Mohammad Davudi; **Editor:** Hassan Hassandust; **Sound:** Yadollah Najafi; **Main Cast:** Mohsen Ramezani, Hossein Mahjoub.

The Colour of Pomegranates (*Sayat Nova*)
Soviet Union, 1969 – 79 mins
Sergei Paradjanov

Ornately based on episodic chapters in the life of the Armenian poet
Sayat Nova, *The Colour of Pomegranates* is framed, staged and
performed like a poem. Not a single incident of prose is cast on its
audiovisual screen; not a single photographic event is hung within its
pictorial catacombs. Its world is poetic from earth to sky and dust to sea
– not in any meagre metaphorical sense but in a heightened iconic sense.
Just as the icon in Orthodox religious dogma is a testament to that which
cannot be represented so great is its presence, iconic presentation
governs the mode of all occurrences in the film.

   Richness of sound, image and gesture is so potent in *The Colour of
Pomegranates* that a strange synaesthetic giddiness overtakes the film.
Everything is tactile, edible, fragrant, sensual, arousing. It is as if we are
inhabiting the being of Sayat-Nova as his life is charted across the film's
fifteen movements. We take in and savour each and every impression
which led him down his path of poetic consciousness. This is another
reinforcement of the film's disavowal of mimetic operations: Sayat-
Nova's very senses are the brush, quill, ink and papyrus of the film's
audiovisual text (all being key elements he is indoctrinated as a child to
love). Spices, plaster, goldleaf, blood, sand, feathers, silk, sweat, ash,
steam, fruit, brass, metal, wax, dye, alabaster, tiles – a universe of
decorative paraphernalia and ritual accoutrements are displayed in
ethnographic gravure; museographic without being necrophiliac; natural
while being ritual.

   The *Colour of Pomegranates* achieves this sublimation of
viewer/auditor into the poet's psyche by a measured and consistent
attunement to gestural declaration and metrical placement. Breathing
the phrasing of Sayat-Nova's poems (which when ungainly staggered as
intertitles somewhat disrupts this effect), the film arranges sound and
image in proportion to their textual evocation within the poems'

structure. On-screen and off-screen sounds – be they spot effects or continuous atmospheres – are thus flattened in a layer of significance, unmodulated and unmodified. Sung refrains, chanted prayers, murmured incantations are similarly streamed into fixed discursive lines, sometimes brutishly syncing to visible characters, other times floating across visual montages like an ethereal broadcast. Musical eddies are cupped, irrigated and evaporated with total fluidity, spilling across faces and floating past bodies.

Lyrical to a sublime level, *The Colour of Pomegranates* subscribes to the phenomenological status of the aural as being that which cannot be anything but itself. The cry of a peacock may represent any number of things, but its sound is wholly that and that alone. The image of a peacock, by comparison, is but the collective rabble of versions, interpretations and understandings of that which it might be. The film's poetic titular conundrum is a key to understanding its iconic logic, for there is no name for the colour of pomegranates except the colour that has to be experienced in order to recognise it. Whether one agrees or not with the philosophical thrust of these icon-privileging claims, *The Colour of Pomegranates* cherishes and savours them greatly.

Dir: Sergei Paradjanov; **Prod:** uncredited; **Scr:** Sergei Paradjanov; **DOP:** Martyn Shakhbazyan, Suren Shakhbazyan; **Editor:** Sergei Paradzhanov; **Score:** Tigran Mansuryan; **Sound:** uncredited; **Main Cast:** Sofiko Chiavreli, Melkon Aleksanyan, Vilen Galstyan, Georgi Gegechkory, Onik Minasyan.

(Next page) The Colour of Pomegranates: not a single incident of prose upon its audiovisual screen

Contact
US, 1997 – 144 mins
Robert Zemeckis

Contact opens with a visualisation of much we could never see, but most of which we have heard. What at first appears to be a gratuitous computer-generated track through space is in fact an astronomical journey through sonic time capsules, dotted across outer space in a line that documents the moments of their emission. A wash of song and noise is jettisoned through the screen's frontal zones and spurts into the rear surround sound field. The direction of the dynamics becomes clear: we are not travelling into outer space; we are listening from outer space. *Contact* inverts audiovisual relationships as key leverage for proposing the realignment of cultural, textual and even mystical precepts. This scene is a suggestion not of who we as central beings are in contact with, but who from beyond may contact us.

Contact's central figure, Ellie Arroway (Foster) is from the beginning searching for something: an unjustifiable existence which she cannot see. Crucially, she is not interested in the encoding of a past event: she scans the airwaves in the present, fishing for sonic signals that intersect her receiver across radically displaced zones of time and place. She replaces the camera and the microphone with radar. She does not wish to 'find out' something; she wants to find something – directly, unmediated, unconditionally. If astronomical charts outline what exists where, Ellie's obsessively pin-covered charts outline what might exist but doesn't reside at each pin point.

Many rich images in *Contact* affirm this, as Ellie closes off her terrestrial world while plugged into another realm, erotically lulled by a continuum of noise spitting through her headphones. Just as her space maps grow in scale and density, so too do her ears: from a single set of headphones to the earth-shaking moment when she commands a phalanx of gigantic satellite dishes to rotate in sync with her as she rushes in a pick-up truck to snare the location point of an extraterrestrial sonic emission.

When she finally makes contact, a dimensional pulsation grows which sonically invades the auditorium. As auditors, looking at a spectral analyser with its pumping LEDs while hearing this sound, we occupy the fused headphonic/radarphonic space of Ellie: a primed and imaginative place where the desire to hear external presences creates the net wherein signs of the beyond can roost. Here, surround sound activity precisely captures all that the screen cannot show. If we are to be contacted by something beyond – as postulated in much sci-fi writing – it will first make us realise the limited recording range of both our mental facilities and monitoring technologies.

The complex phenomenological and technological ramifications of *Contact*'s hypothesis mark it a first in employing surround spatialisation not merely for Judeo-Christian spookery, but for the investigation of how one shifts from a centred existence to a decentred one. *Contact*'s mystical pondering is broad enough not to be thematically rooted in either religious or humanist dogma, and open enough to state the vitality of sound as a life force whose energy fields and physical expansiveness affect us deeply despite the thinness of our ocular rationalism.

Dir: Robert Zemeckis; **Prod:** Steve Starkey, Robert Zemeckis; **Scr:** Carl Sagan, Ann Druyan, James V. Hart, Michael Goldenberg; **DOP:** Don Burgess; **Editor:** Arthur Schmidt; **Score:** Alan Silvestri; **Sound Design:** Randy Thom; **Main Cast:** Jodie Foster, Mathew McConaughey, David Morse, Tom Skerritt.

The Convent (O Convento)
Portugal, 1998 – 94 mins
Manoel De Oliveira

An astoundingly perplexing text, there may be many entirely mismatched ways to describe *The Convent*. The 'plot' is simple enough. To aid his research on the true genealogy of Shakespeare, Michael (Malkovich) arrives at a ruined convent with his wife Helene (Deneuve). There they are greeted by Baltar (Cintra), who presents Michael with a research assistant, Piedade (Silveira). Baltar is hoping that Piedade will seduce Michael, while he himself attempts to seduce Michael's wife Helene. A strung-out bourgeois chamber drama, for certain. Yet *The Convent* erupts in a rash of emotional boils due to its powerfully possessive music.

Replaying select and (in most instances) unedited movements from Sofia Gubajdulina's *Offertorium – The Seven Last Words* and Igor Stravinsky's *The Rake's Progress*, *The Convent* threads these works' gorgeous atonality to overwhelm the superficial trappings of the characters, and entangle them in the music's psychological penumbra. First impressions will likely confound, caused by the stinging effect of what appears to be misplaced and inappropriate orchestral incursions. These taint the actors with laughable melodrama, refusing to match their projection and stature. The characters seem to be rendered as defaced statues with incomprehensible expressions on their faces – just like those that populate the convent's surroundings.

Yet it is through the action of replaying these movements that one discerns their purpose and deeper effect on the film's visible action. As cued from its first manifestation, the music is not aligned with character as one presumes: it comes from within the metaphysical spaces that comprise the convent. Gates, doorways, caves, grottoes, chapels and quarters are continually framed from the inside, looking out at those who peer into their indigo ambience. As Baltar and his assistants are seen to be practising satanists (of a decidedly reserved order) into whose necromantic hands the convent has been entrusted, the convent's sacred sanctity is recognised more as a Jurassic battlefield between good and evil. Once Piedade and Baltar each start quoting Goethe's *Faust* (and the film obliquely quotes *Nosferatu*), each starts shaping Michael and Helene into players on a Faustian stage. The role of Gubajdulina's and Stravinsky's music instates *The Convent* with a multiplicity of metaphysical assertions on the blurring between good and evil, as their excerpts' atonality is liberated from overt description and emotional registration.

As the film closes and each of the characters has literally disappeared (Baltar and Piedade into an abyss deep in the Witch's Forest; Michael and Helene into the 'giant vulva' of a cave which houses an ancient chapel despite its volcanic formation as one of Satan's original furnaces), the music similarly withdraws, leaving us with the sound of ocean waves lapping at the characters' absence.

Dir: Manoel De Oliveira; **Prod:** Paul Branco; **Scr:** Manoel De Oliveira; **DOP:** Mário Barroso; **Editor:** Valérie Loiseleux, Manoel De Oliveira; **Sourced Score:** Igor Stravinsky, Sofiya Gubajdulina, Toshir Mayazumi; **Sound:** Jean-Paul Mugel; **Main Cast:** Catherine Deneuve, John Malkovich, Luis Miguel Cintra, Leonor Silveira.

The Conversation
US, 1974 – 113 mins
Francis Ford Coppola

The Conversation sculpts a mindscape of piercing interiority which demonstrates how complex and effective noise can be in detailing shifting mental states. That's 'noise' in both sonic and psychological senses: interference, distortion, unfidelity, overload – all the tactile signifiers of the moment when sound becomes its Other, its nightmare, its transfigured monster.

Repressed and near-dysfunctional Harry Caul (Hackman) is a solipsistic sound recordist bent on tapping other people's private conversations – a perfect vehicle to drive a character whose stability is maintained by treating dialogue purely as legible sonic data. But when Harry reads meaning into the recorded dialogue, pure sound becomes oppressive noise, representing the impenetrability of both the tape he has recorded and the psychological wall he has built around his sense of self. Many stirring moments are founded on the aesthetics of ring modulation, sweep equalisation and inverted compression ratios, but never are they employed as decoration. The story brings the noise as the drama demands it, figuring the soundtrack as a resolutely tailored text with little concern for gratuitous kooky sound effects typically employed to illustrate someone losing their mind.

The inner emptiness of Harry is not unlike a studio whose acoustic character has been deadened. Sonic alarms control the perimeter of his sealed fortress; a silent number blocks incoming calls. He amplifies his loneliness, making his solitude deafening. For therapy, he plays saxophone solos on top of a live jazz recording, pausing at the right moments to acknowledge the pre-recorded applause. Even the camera pans across this space indifferently, as if he is not there. Harry's workspace is similarly void of presence: a cavernous warehouse with a small locked cage where his specially constructed recording and decoding equipment is gathered into one controlled zone. And not surprisingly, his

The Conversation: the recorder becomes the recorded

affair with Amy (Garr) is based on similar control over her, boxing her in and rendering their relationship invisible and silent.

Being invisible through silence is Harry's mode of self-statement: he prides himself on not being heard while hearing others – hence his outrage at being bugged by Stan (John Cazale) in a rare moment of tenderness with Lurleen (Phoebe Alexander). For Harry, interference is largely a challenge – something to filter out, reduce and sublimate. But interference becomes a devastating affair when outsiders rupture his space by perceiving its invisibility. When Harry himself is bugged, his world falls apart absolutely. His isolation booth of an apartment is torn asunder as he wrecks walls, floors, ceiling and fittings trying to uncover the tapping device. This truly is someone having their world turned inside out, as the recorder becomes the recorded. Encoded as data for others after so desperately defining himself through the appropriation of others' data, his sonic visage becomes a frail actuality: his self is noted by others, being both the thing he most desires and that which will destroy him. Playing his sax in destitution surrounded by the rubble of his space, a reversal takes hold of his sonic psyche: he now hears himself as he hears others.

Dir: Francis Ford Coppola; **Prod:** Francis Ford Coppola; **Scr:** Francis Ford Coppola; **DOP:** Bill Butler; **Editor:** Richard Chew, Walter Murch; **Score:** David Shire; **Sound Design:** Walter Murch; **Main Cast:** Gene Hackman, Frederic Forrest, Cindy Williams, Terri Garr, Harrison Ford, Robert Duvall.

Crash
Canada, 1996 – 100 mins
David Cronenberg

Crash is a complex film in its choice to depict polysexual states and
sensibilities. Counter to most options picked up in both legitimate and
porn cinema, *Crash* is concerned with moving past the body, beyond its
organic states and conditions, into the uncharted realm of paraphilia:
that state, literally, 'beyond love', where the erotic is displaced and the
sexual reconfigured by the most unlikely of triggers and stimuli. This
means that traditional images of the body on screen are placed there
primarily for the purpose of moving through them. *Crash*'s score is
similarly deceptive: it appears to have a slight modern tonality on its
shimmering, amplified surface, what with electric guitars combined with
harp and prepared piano. But the score is more concerned with
composing appropriately for the polysexual condition of *Crash*'s story by
transcending the obviousness of 'radical' tonalities.

The score splits its orchestration into two sections: the guitars/harps
and the woodwinds. Throughout the film, the central theme literally
morphs between the two, so that the woodwinds remind one of the
guitars no longer present, and vice versa. This absenting of singular
musical character dryly complements the emptying of identity in the
conventional sexual act. As innocent and hyper-softly spoken James
Ballard (Spader) wafts into a new terrain of sexuality prompted by his
encounters with his wife Catherine (Unger), Helen Rimmington (Hunter),
Gabrielle (Arquette) and others, bodies appear to be as they were before,
but they now contain a distinct Otherness. They shine like chrome; smell
like vinyl; feel like leather; sound like an engine.

Just as the history of film scoring for the sexual act is a history of
covering bodily noise and creating a surfeit of unnecessary narration to
compensate for the embarrassing images shown, *Crash*'s score is a
genteel acceptance of the aural fading of that same musical cloaking.
Musicologically, *Crash* addresses that perverse audiovisual dilemma of

cinema: what music should formally occupy the soundtrack in accompaniment to the sounds and images of bodies having sex? Counter to the mysterious fade to black or the rapid shuttle to the lurid symbolism of fireworks and crashing waves, the visualisation of the sexual act necessitated previously unimagined aural accompaniment.

While a plethora of resulting musical scores have generated perplexing conventions that highlight the fissures between the image-track's conscious narration and the soundtrack's liminal operation, *Crash* redefines this procedeure by composing music for openly aroused emotional states. In a number of scenes where James wanders through a hellish panorama of car-crash debris and human remains, the score highlights his arousal in place of any expected pathos, harmonically dissolving slightly mournful progressions into luxuriously thickened instrumentation. The 'beauty in death' connoted here is not simply a Romantic affectation, but a severely sexual condition.

Crash sits between the luridly Romantic and the aggressively pornographic. Hard-core porn's unique solution to how to score sex acts has resulted in a blatant disregard for combining appropriate music with ocular gynaecological pursuits, rendering its films' music surreal and unsettling. Soft-core porn's mock-Euro attributes characterise its films as desperate and deluded in their pretence to sensitivity, while hammering sexual gyrations with a cinematic sledge hammer. *Crash* can be viewed as a psychological and musical accident site where all these pre-existing codes of representation have collided. Seriously contemplating appropriate musical accompaniment to moments like Gabrielle in calipers rubbing her scarred flesh against the bonnet of an expensive car in a showroom, it redefines the erotic in music.

Dir: David Cronenberg; **Prod:** David Cronenberg; **Scr:** David Cronenberg; **DOP:** Peter Suschitzky; **Editor:** Ronald Sanders; **Score:** Howard Shore; **Sound Effects Supervision:** David Evans; **Main Cast:** James Spader, Holly Hunter, Elias Koteas, Deborah Unger, Rosanna Arquette.

Crazy
Netherlands, 1999 – 97 mins
Heddy Honigmann

In *Crazy*, soldiers, aid-workers and counsellors who have spent military duty and/or peacekeeping time in places like Seoul, Saigon, Phnom Penh, Lebanon, Kosovo and Rwanda are interviewed about what songs they cherished from their time spent in those places, and what memories the songs bring back. Then, in a recall of the camera gaze shared by Warhol and Akerman, we watch their faces as they listen to the songs. The beauty of the film is not in its humanist celebration of the will to survive beyond the ravages of such hellish experiences, but in its foregrounding of how song – in its most consumerist guise and outright commodification – can transcend the damning critiques pop music tends to attract.

The film opens with the phased churning of a chopper intermingling with strains of the Three Tenors singing 'Nessun Dorma' (from the Puccini opera *Turandot*). Of course, *Apocalypse Now* is evoked by this clash of beauty with death. But in *Crazy*, it is revealed that 'Nessun Dorma' is less a musical projectile and more an aural impression mapped by the face that listens to it. As we watch an ex-soldier listen to one of the 80s' most kitsch grotesqueries of high-art super-group bellowing, it is as if the pores of his skin 'become' the laser-burnt pits of the CD recording. The surface of his face shows only the slightest quivering in response to the sound waves of the music as it fills his being. Eyes open, occasionally blinking, audibly breathing, he – like most of *Crazy*'s subjects – does not fit the desired romanticised quasi-religious icon of the ecstatic listener, enthralled by harmonic rapture with eyes wide shut. His face is removed, ungiving, transported. The effect is undeniable: we bear witness to the phonological materiality of the song as inscription; as that which is listened to rather than that which is encoded, recorded, produced or performed. The transparent psychosonic skin that wavers between objectivity (the song as music) and subjectivity (the song as experience) shimmers and fluctuates.

The laying of music 'on top of' someone's face on a screen can not only project an emotional reading of the character's state of mind, but can also externalise the interiority of the imagined person. *Crazy* outrightly documents this. Each song states: I am what is inside this head, behind this face, within this listener. *Crazy* also proves absolutely that any narrative can embrace any song for any purpose. It evidences music – in the receptacle of songs – as an uncontrollable force, both from the songwriter/singer's intention and in the film subjects' reception of the song. The ex-soldiers all fix their songs to precise incidents and moments which did not call for the songs that fused themselves to their listeners. Music – as one guy puts it in the film – is 'weird stuff'. In the end, all the songs perform as a talisman against the craziness in which they found themselves gradually sinking. *Crazy's* minimalist documentary technique is a testament not merely to the human spirit, but to the power of song.

Dir: Heddy Honigmann; **Prod:** Pieter Van Huystee; **Scr:** Heddy Honigmann; **DOP:** Gregor Meerman; **Editor:** Mario Steenbergen; **Sourced Songs:** Giacomo Puccini, Elvis Presley, Seal, Guns N' Roses, U2; **Sound Editor:** Hugo Dijkstal.

Days of Wine and Roses
US, 1962 – 117 mins
Blake Edwards

The bitter-sweet music of *Days of Wine and Roses* embodies a moving study of Joe Clay (Lemmon) and Kirsten Arnesen's (Remick) 'marriage on the rocks'. The score exemplifies a counter-trend in American film music where an identifiable pop song replaces the Wagnerian leitmotiv as a principle of construction. Close inspection of *Days of Wine and Roses'* score uncovers an unusual chameleon-like make-up in its arrangements. Presumed to be 'pop', the transformation of the cues' reworking of the title theme constitutes a thoroughly modern serialism – not at the incremental diatonic substrata, but at the plateau of pop form. This bizarre structural cross-hatching of Schoenberg and Bacharach sites the active layers and levels of the music not within its composition per se, but more in its orchestration. The movement through these modular, decentred and fractured versions musically narrates the social and emotional descent of Joe and Kirsten into alcoholism.

The opening credits present the title song with lyrics, sung in decorously drippy male and female harmonies. Somewhere between slowed-down Swingle Singers and woozy Modernaires, the melodiousness of their fawned lilts and sighing crescendos prepares one for melodrama. But such a recourse is never taken. Rather, the vocal version is a set-up: a garish humanist billboard behind whose shadows exists the world of the film with its post-noir moral murkiness and its proto-sociological advocation of Alcoholics Anonymous. All proceeding music follows the pattern established by the elaborate yet subtle suite of thematic variations which play under Joe and Kirsten's first date. Having eased into the other's familiarity, they sit at the dock of the bay, Joe buoyant by bourbon, Kirsten bubbling from her first brandy Alexander. Luminescence from the water below flickers on their faces as they open up to each other. The theme synchronously melts into a distended solo

Days of Wine and Roses: distended solo lines and strung-out themes

line without backing. The jazz-intoned harmonies and chromatic shifts in the melody are now rendered atonal and alien, as their raw and exposed dreams, ambitions and memories emotionally fuse.

This approach is then variegated with great sensitivity to the drama. When Joe thinks he sees a 'bum' in the street – but then realises he has caught his reflection in a bar window – the theme collapses into fleshy folds around its skeletal melody. When he is sedated by force in a sanatorium as his body is being overcome by alcoholic poisoning, his eyes glaze as the theme is contorted into a DNA model of its former self. The deeper Joe and Kirsten slide into addiction, the more 'strung-out' the theme becomes. Oppositely, when chordal support is draped around the title melody, it corresponds to moments in Joe and Kirsten's consciousness of their situation. They see glimmers of their former selves; the music recalls the warmth conveyed in its initial vocal arrangement. Amazingly, the film sadly concludes with a softly intoned sole note played on French horn as Kirsten walks away alone, typifying the extent to which the score has actioned its own 'harmonic being' as the means for writing its elegy.

Dir: Blake Edwards; **Prod:** Martin Manulis; **Scr:** J. P. Miller; **DOP:** Philip H. Lathrop; **Editor:** Patrick McCormack; **Score:** Henry Mancini; **Sound:** Jack Solomon; **Main Cast:** Jack Lemmon, Lee Remick, Charles Bickford, Jack Klugman.

Dead Man
US, 1995 – 121 mins
Jim Jarmusch

If the soundtrack as we know it had never been developed – if it had never concretely and technically locked sound to image – film music now might be like it is in *Dead Man*. Performed by non-film composer Neil Young mostly in real-time passages to edited scenes solely on electric guitar, its music is neither scored nor conducted. Quite the opposite, it scores image by folding its tones across the visuals, and conducts energy through electrified means. It literally plugs into the images and amplifies them, reading its performers like a shaman reading a liver. The music responds to its locations by sounding that which is invisible to its inhabitants.

A complete inversion of mythic, heroic and romantic Westerns, *Dead Man* follows William Blake (Depp), an accountant from Cleveland who travels to the perversely named Machine to work for a steel mill, but ends up being accidentally shot and set loose into the wild woods. As itinerant and wandering as the film's Homeric odyssey, *Dead Man*'s music idly dances around its images and sequences, never making bold statements, never formulating a structure, never making overt sense of that which it appears to describe. The guitar acknowledges the film's status as mystical Western, its alienation from itself via tube distortion and room reverb echoing the existential landscape traversed by William Blake as he slowly dies from within as a bullet poisons his being.

Introduced as recognisable motifs – braced by an acoustic guitar overlay during the title credits – variations on the guitar's themes and its chord progressions become more fractured as William Blake's life force seeps. Blake is befriended and guided on a spiritual journey by the Indian Nobody (Farmer), becoming closer to death as he nears the ocean, where he is eventually set loose in a canoe. As the waves carry him away, the guitar throbs like a heart's final pulsation. The final ocean journey recalls Blake's original travel deep into the American woods by train. Through a dotted line of narcoleptic black-outs, Blake attempts to remain composed as the world around him progressively transforms into a realm of animalistic beings, morbid behaviour and nightmarish landscapes. Upon arriving at Machine – a din-ridden industrialised Hades whose Vulcanite machines signal the death of the Old World in the face of noisy greed – this Cleveland accountant finds no welcome quarter. He has entered a lost world from which he will not return. The palpably 'live' electric guitar charts his nervous fluctuations, his shifts in consciousness, his receptiveness to unworldly traits, and his final acceptance that William Blake is indeed a dead man.

Dir: Jim Jarmusch; **Prod:** Demetra J. Macbride; **Scr:** Jim Jarmusch; **DOP:** Robby Muller; **Editor:** Jay Rabinowitz; **Score:** Neil Young; **Supervising Sound Editor:** Robert Hein; **Main Cast:** Johnny Depp, Gary Farmer, Lance Henriksen, Michael Wincott, Robert Mitchum.

Distant Thunder (*Ashani Sanket*)
India, 1973 – 100 mins
Satyajit Ray

A work of remarkable restraint, *Distant Thunder* is as quiet as the
Bollywood musical is loud. But this is not a value judgment typical of the
wedges driven to separate Hindi art films from Masala musicals: the
binary of quiet/loud does not equate good/bad. The softness of *Distant
Thunder* relates to a dramaturgical stratagem whose aural awareness is
marked in the film's sonic grain.

The first distinctive feature of sound in *Distant Thunder* is its
ethnographic ambience. An overlooked aspect of much non-Western
cinema is how a culture's domestic architecture affects a film's staging.
Theatre's traditional proscenium is based on a room-with-a-view – which
is fine if you spend most time (and most of your familial conflict) indoors.
But cultures who live and work predominantly outside or with open
doors have no need for the invisible fourth wall of the proscenium's
paradigm. Sound design in service to naturalism is then forced to
acknowledge that there is no sound for the 'inside' of a room due to all
the 'outside' sound leaking in. This is undoubtedly a guiding principle for
Distant Thunder's sound: all manner of insect and bird life is continually
audible. Post-dubbed and planar in their blunt occupancy of the
soundtrack, these sounds nonetheless relate to a specific acoustic field of
reference – Indian rural life.

This apparent naturalism of sound is crucial to setting up *Distant
Thunder* as a slight documentary-tinged study. But this veneer peels
away as *Distant Thunder*'s story unfolds. Set during World War II, it
follows the plight of husband and wife Gangacharan (Chatterjee) and
Ananga (Babita) as their life is slowly changed by global situations which
initially seem to be far removed from their near-subsistence living. The
sound that signifies the encroaching global forces is that of war planes
flying overheard in formation. At first, the sound of the planes is a
thrilling novelty. Later, they signify aberrant transgression when Babita's

screams are drowned by their volume as she is raped while her girlfriends scan the skies to spot the planes. Eventually, the deep hum of the flying machines represents an intrusive terror which grips everyone as the Bengal famine spreads and takes hold of the village. The once-distant thunder is now a deadly drone.

The tactile ambience of Gangacharan and Ananga's life is mostly rich in detail: heat, wind, river water, dusty ground, tree trunks, rustling leaves, floating fabric, colourful spices – all are portrayed simultaneously as fragile yet vibrant signs of life. Their accompanying sounds are accorded similar respect not for an isolated celebration of Nature's beauty, but to intensify the accruing loss which leads Gangacharan, Ananga and those around them down a brutal path of existence. A simplistic yet sensual score is woven into this ambience, whose central theme's melodic lilt is ultimately mournful. With aching majesty, it builds in proportion to the dwindling of the sounds of life as the village withers; beaten into submission by planes which drop no bombs, but whose fatal thunder darkens the villagers' sky.

Dir: Satyajit Ray; **Prod:** Sharbani Bhattacharya; **Scr:** Bibhutibhushan Bandyopadhyay, Satyajit Ray; **DOP:** Soumendu Roy; **Editor:** Dulal Dutta; **Score:** Satyajit Ray; **Sound:** J. D. Irani, Durgadas Mitra; **Main Cast:** Babita, Chitra Banerjee, Govinda Chakravarti, Soumitra Chatterjee.

Do the Right Thing
US, 1989 – 94 mins
Spike Lee

A camera crane glides up, lifting us through the tops of maple trees,
resting on a view of houses and apartments with stoops rolling down to
street level. It looks like the mythical New York residential street shot on
Universal's 'Main Street' lot for the past fifty years. Lush, orchestrated
strings convey the sensation of rising, floating, hovering. The fuzzy
homespun blanket of classical Hollywood Americana is harmonically
spun. But this is a real street in Bedford Stuyvesant, New York. The film is
Do the Right Thing and the score is contemporary.

Something is wrong with this picture. Why is a radically black film
resorting to white picturesque music? Because this music – that lilting
brave tonality of epic Americana – is not white. It is a dense harmonic
cartography of America's racial and colonial history. It contains hymnal
strains of Baptist eulogies, shifting undertones of transient blues idioms,
metamorphosing key changes typical of jazz arrangements. This music –
despite its accrued signage of white Hollywood humanism – is black.

To comprehend and identify this germ of blackness, one must
audibly trace its major carriers: the 'new world' sound of symphonic
works by Virgil Thomson and Aaron Copland. *Do the Right Thing*'s score
might appear to be a jazz-quotation of classical Hollywood music, but its
line of reference goes straight to the corpus of Thomson and Copland.
Their triumphant yet melancholic compositions reside in the popular
consciousness as sublime icons of America's majestic land mass, and
have an uncanny effect of atonement when set to images of America's
abuse of its land and people. Thomson's scores for documentaries about
the harshness of the land were highly influential in imbuing farmers'
struggles with pathos via his embrace of blues, folk and ethnic music to
characterise his harmonies with non-European modals. Copland worked
in a less quotative and more transformative manner with his
Americanesque ballets and symphonies, yet imbedded deep in his

Do the Right Thing: music as a cartography of racial and colonial history

climbing 4ths and 5ths are the templates of blues chord progressions – clearly audible in his unsentimental accompaniment to *Of Mice and Men*'s (1939) depiction of Depression-era America.

Of course, land ownership and territorial possession are regenerated to form the crux of *Do the Right Thing*: who owns what, who takes from whom, who inhabits where. The score reclaims that melancholic sound like forty acres of harmony and replays it as a contemporary racial threnody – one that poignantly breathes between the tenser moments of conflict between the Italians, Koreans and African Americans. Operating as much at an ideological level as a musical level, this amounts to a socio-political perspective on the possession and authorship of harmony and melody in film music. The outré politicisation of *Do the Right Thing* is most readily apparent in the presence of Radio Raheem (Nunn) blasting hip hop into social spaces and onto the film's soundtrack in an act of territorial transgression. But one is wise not to be deaf to the film's quieter carpet of urban pastoralism. For just as so many key 'Americana' composers openly or obliquely referenced black folk/popular music as a strategy for defining an American identity against European affectation, *Do the Right Thing* explores first-degree folk/popular music as the material from which to mould a soundtrack as an act of reclamation.

Dir: Spike Lee; **Prod:** Spike Lee; **Scr:** Spike Lee; **DOP:** Ernest Dickerson; **Editor:** Barry Alexander Brown; **Score:** Bill Lee; **Songs:** Public Enemy; **Sound Design:** Skip Lievsay; **Main Cast:** Danny Aiello, Ossie Davis, Spike Lee, Bill Nunn, John Turturro, Rosie Perez.

Dr. Dolittle
US, 1998 – 85 mins
Betty Thomas

Dr. Dolittle (Murphy) says a very telling line in the remake of *Dr. Dolittle*: 'I'll end up like one of those people on the streets talking to themselves. It ain't a good look.' The film goes as far as having Eddie Murphy interred in a psychiatric hospital because he claims he can talk to the animals. The film soon becomes hopelessly trapped by its own contradictory do-gooding, for at the end of the day, no one is going to believe anyone can talk to the animals and hear exactly what they say.

The more that vocalised schizophrenia takes hold of the urban audiopolis, the more we will try to deny it, and the louder its noise will get. Every time we ignore that person talking to themselves, the more we socially enforce a cone of silence which actually allows the person with schizophrenia to expand their 'acoustic personal space'. They figure our silence is an acceptance of their expanded aural territorialisation. That is the key role we as 'non-crazies' play in increasing the city's audible threshold.

In *Dr. Dolittle*, the term 'schizophrenia' is never mentioned, but it is screamed non-stop throughout the subliminal terrain of the film's soundtrack. Like a mega mix of the soundtracks to *The Adventures of Milo and Otis* (1986), *Look Who's Talking* (1989) and *Babe* (1995), a thousand and one wannabe comedians desperately vie for your attention on screen and off screen with their smarmy wisecracks. Listening to *Dr. Dolittle*'s living and dead stuffed animals with digitally composited lip movements is cacophonous, pathetic, scary. It is noise at its most fundamental: the collapse of communication through overload; the inverting of interiority; the ultimate surrounding of sound.

The soundtrack to *Dr. Dolittle* is less a matter of crafted sound design and more an almost accidental intersection between socio-acoustics from the outside world and psychoacoustics inside the sanctity of the cinema. This marks the film as a rare case in the way that its soundtrack reflects how vocal noise on the street bears little relation to the formal ways in which the recording and placement of voice has become part of film language. The value of *Dr. Dolittle* then is socially therapeutic: it gives pause to consider the exclusivity with which film language denies aberrant communication which we hear most days when we walk down the street.

The complex audiovisual distancing employed by people wishing to ignore 'street crazies' is itself a form of 'reality mixing'. The ability with which 'clinically sane' citizens can filter out noise for the sake of their own sanity is amazing. For whenever one hears the floating voices of others' schizophrenia, one is hearing the potential advance echo of one's own demise. Following the premise that comedy arises from the misfortune of others, *Dr. Dolittle* is listed as being a comedy. Maybe the aural moral is: laugh while you can.

Dir: Betty Thomas; **Prod:** John Davis, David T. Friendly, Joseph Singer; **Scr:** Nat Mauldin, Larry Levin; **DOP:** Russell Boyd; **Editor:** Peter Teschner; **Score:** Richard Gibbs; **Sound Design:** John A. Larsen; **Main Cast:** Eddie Murphy, Ossie Davis, Oliver Platt, Peter Boyle.

Escape from New York
US, 1981 – 99 mins
John Carpenter

In the predominantly bombastic world of cinema, a score featuring the repetition of a single note is unlikely. It may also be unlikely that Manhattan will be turned into a sealed-off prison where homicidal killers are left to govern themselves, prevented from escaping across the island's dynamite-laden bridges. *Escape from New York* proposes this and enshrines the sustaining of a single note as its primary device for modulating tension.

Played by synthesiser banks triggered by sequencers, the pulse is exceedingly inhuman. Metronomically controlled by voltage instead of wind-up mechanisms, tonally shaped from oscillators instead of acoustic materials, pitched by frequency controls instead of malleable tuning, the sound of music in *Escape from New York* is never actual. Rather, it is the by-product of electrical energy – always stated and presented as such and never allowed to 'become music'. This particular approach to synthesiser composition and performance constitutes an act of 'descoring' for film, in that the synthesiser's innate capacity for 'inhumanness' is exploited to conduct (literally) energy and channel it through the score.

'Descoring' strategically operates through the systematic multi-tracking and programming of synthesiser banks. Parts of the score convey diminution, residua and absence of musical parts and voices. Passages will break down to a single note – sometimes to no more than a Geiger counter clicking. The gradual shrinking of musical activity and sonic layers throughout *Escape from New York* inverts the epic grandeur implicit in actively 'building up' music for the movies.

The urban landscape in *Escape from New York* evokes this: frontier facades, vacated blocks and toppled monuments crumble into each other in unfolding dioramas depicting the demise of a once-great metropolis. As the Duke (Hayes) cruises through the rubble of Manhattan in his

Cadillac adorned with candelabra, a musicological cue of greater import is expressed by the throbbing synthesisers. *Escape from New York* is the *Shaft* (1971) of the future: chugging wah-wah guitars and percolating hi-hats have been reduced to blips and beeps on the musicological radar. Simultaneously, those pulses represent the ticking time-bomb inside Snake (Russell) as he searches for the US President (Pleasence) kidnapped by the Duke, as well as the tracking device attached to the President.

Escape from New York's economical employment of the monophonic pulse becomes the perfect foil for measuring changing degrees of dramatic tension. The score is thus an ECG reading of Snake's drama. Positioned away from melodramatic statement, it is a narratological transposition of minimalism's drone and loop states, where the absence of horizontal melody intensifies one's awareness of the vertical depth in any one note or singular musical fragment. When actual music does appear, it arrives as a battered cassette tape of Dixieland jazz, globally broadcast in place of a vital message from the President to deter an impending world war. Derisively planted by Snake as repayment for the double-crosses he has endured, he walks away unfurling the original tape in a symbolic act of 'decomposition'.

Dir: John Carpenter; **Prod:** Larry J. Franco, Debra Hill; **Scr:** John Carpenter, Nick Castle; **DOP:** Dean Cundey, Jim Lucas; **Editor:** Todd C. Ramsay; **Score:** John Carpenter; **Sound Mix:** Steve Maslow; **Main Cast:** Kurt Russell, Lee Van Cleef, Ernest Borgnine, Donald Pleasence, Isaac Hayes, Harry Dean Stanton, Adrienne Barbeau.

The Exorcist
US, 1971 – 121 mins
William Friedkin

Renowned for its violent imagery, *The Exorcist* unsettles its audience initially through sound, showing us little in the first half of the film. Repeatedly, incisive aural rupture is caused by inordinately loud and disproportionately banal sound edits: a cup smashes, a phone rings, a car horn beeps, a door slams shut. Stretched between each sonar shock, one can hear the soundscape slowly nullify the New England calm – from the destabilising quiet separated mother Chris MacNeil (Burstyn) endures while coming to terms with her divorce, to the intense pauses as her daughter Regan (Blair) waits for a Ouija board to come to life. Before too long, one is put on edge by the viciousness of common sounds while being smothered by a visual domesticity.

The tension between sound and image is crucial to setting us up for the film's forthcoming visceral ocularism. This is not to say the soundtrack is merely the result of an overly deliberated assault to wear down the audience. Quite the opposite: it plays with the audience's relation to the film's naturalistic tone – distinctively low key in its drama – almost as if a Satanic horror film has possessed a family documentary portrait. The visual and aural traits of each respective genre are orchestrated to amplify this change. The first half of *The Exorcist* documents how the comfortable home of Chris and Regan is being transformed into an upside-down simulacrum of Hades. The second half performs identically, but in sole operation upon the body of Regan. Through her, the voice of female pubescence is rendered by a hellish chorus of effects and transmogrifications, and it is here that the soundtrack becomes aberrant and vilifying.

Possessed by a devil, Regan speaks in foreign languages, reversed recordings and diabolical dialogue. Drained of the personal, filled from beyond and fuelled by possession, Regan's whole body becomes a distorted receiver/broadcaster for Satanic power. She is a Ouija body:

letters press outwards from her abdomen to emboss the word 'help' in typographical welts; spinal gymnastics redefine the limits of contortion as her head spins 180 degrees to face those whom she addresses; vulgarities spew forth in linguistic and bilious form until she literally exhales a stream of vomit. As words become abject matter – phlegm for insult, saliva for disdain – the voice becomes an aural anus. It no longer voluntarily speaks, but shits uncontrollably.

The Exorcist conjures a nauseating audiovisual imagining of the loss of one's own voice. Regan is silenced through a severing of her psyche from her vocal chords, forcing her to become a bloated vessel for every possible vocalisation of the Other: social, familial, sexual, physical, spiritual. Father Merrin (von Sydow) recites and recants to retrieve her; words are his tools, a Bible his manual. Somewhere deep in the cavernous corporeal cacophony of those who crowd her being lies Regan – lost in the noise of the Other and prevented from screaming with her own voice.

Dir: William Friedkin; **Prod:** William Peter Blatty; **Scr:** William Peter Blatty; **DOP:** Owen Roizman, Billy Williams; **Editor:** Norman Gay, Evan A. Lottman, Bud S. Smith; **Score:** Jack Nitzsche; **Song:** Mike Oldfield; **Sourced Score:** Krzysztof Penderecki, George Crumb, Anton Webern, Hans Werner Henze; **Special Sound Effects:** Doc Siegel, Ron Nagle; **Sound Editor:** Fred Brown; **Main Cast:** Ellen Burstyn, Max von Sydow, Lee J. Cobb, Jason Miller, Linda Blair.

Face/Off
US, 1997 – 138 mins
John Woo

Kung-fu cinema paradoxically deals with showing body movements designed to be too quick for the eye to see. Filmic mechanics are required to disrupt the post-human abilities of the martial artist, reconfigure it into a digestible physiological spatio-temporal continuum, and edit it so that it appears to be happening at an inhuman rate. Running laterally to the jump-cut in Eurocentric dramatic cinema, the jump-cut in Hong Kong action cinema is predicated on this bizarre two-steps-backwards/three-steps-forwards conundrum of depiction.

Face/Off stands as a contemporary landmark in grabbing those sonic moments between the cut and blasting them into the cinesonic ethersphere. Shot after shot, non-fu performers Sean Archer (Travolta) and Castor Troy (Cage) exit the frame only to re-enter the next shot in a way that even Jet Li would find difficult to execute. At these precise moments, the soundtrack blasts one with a whole artillery of orchestral, synthetic and incendiary sound effects. They shoot across the surround-sound space, creating breath-taking maps of plotted action which confuse one into feeling that the screen bodies have in fact performed the feat your eyes did not believe.

In an apt fusion of culture (Peking Opera) with technology (Dolby Surround), *Face/Off* exploits the clarity, definition and sheer volume of full-frequency surround sound to create these spectacular sonic fireworks. Their explosiveness deliberately distracts one from the visuals in a rush of milliseconds where theatre-space – the sculpted sound field you inhabit in the cinema – becomes a sonar hall of mirrors, refracting sound effects, aural devices and musical conventions. Bullet-cam shots are matched by booming tunnels of wind rushes which soar to the rear of the cinema like jets passing overhead at an aviation pageant. Grossly clichéd slo-mo hugs of children on sepia-toned carousels are matched by syrupy stings of glockenspiels which reverberate throughout the

Face/Off: hi-tech Chinese circus music and audiovisual combustion

auditorium. Tex-Mex church shoot-outs and stand-offs are matched by diffused swirls of pigeon flaps and digital choirs. And – best of all – guns fired in aircraft hangars and metallic prison halls are matched by high-transient full-impact bullet ricochets which punctuate the side and rear walls of the theatre with such velocity that one flinches and ducks.

The often violent detachment of these sounds from the image-track posits them as cornerstones in a scene's audiovisual narration. Each of these moments is the result of extensive post-production labour and a purposeful use of psychoacoustics, combined so as not to enhance visuals, disrupt space, or synchronise action. Rather, the sound design of *Face/Off* is appositely engineered to compensate visuals, conjure space and generate action. As a form of cinematised kung-fu, the film's momentum of sound is a hi-tech rush of Chinese circus music: crashing cymbals and swelling gongs, sparkling fire-crackers and booming fire-balls, swishing blades and clanging metal sheets. True to its flashy, showy entertainment, *Face/Off* embodies much that destabilises the naturalistic mimeticism of cinema while exposing the unending attraction of audiovisual combustion.

Dir: John Woo; **Prod:** Terence Chang, Christopher Godsick, Barrie M. Osborne, David Permut; **Scr:** Mike Werb, Michael Colleary; **DOP:** Oliver Wood; **Editor:** Steven Kemper, Christian Wagner; **Score:** John Powell; **Sound Design:** Per Hallberg, Michael A. Reagan, Mark P. Stoeckinger; **Main Cast:** John Travolta, Nicolas Cage, Joan Allen, Alessandro Nivola, Gina Gershon.

Fantasia – The Sorcerer's Apprentice
US, 1940 – 9 mins
James Algar

The first image of *The Sorcerer's Apprentice* (one section of *Fantasia*) is the Sorcerer conjuring shape and form out of vaporous nothingness. Mickey conversely inhabits a physical body in a physical world whose reality is restricted by worldly forces. Perversely, it is a cartoon that is conveying this – and doing so through its literalisation of the symbolism inherent in Paul Dukas' symphonic work *The Sorcerer's Apprentice*. Furthermore, this literalisation is represented by the prime metaphysical conveyor of sound and music: water.

As Mickey falls asleep, the transition from reality to dream centres on the motion of conducting: Mickey is waving his arms to and fro, simultaneously conducting the ethereal forces which energise the broom and the musical energies which dynamise the soundtrack. Soon enough, Mickey awakens into a nightmare, as the abstract sensations he experienced in his dream resulted from physical sensations: Mickey was having a wet dream. The 'reality' of those triggers now confronts Mickey: the speed and intensity of fluidity is now experienced as the movement of liquid out of control in the whirlpool, a liquid vertigo. The music starts swirling and spinning, simulating a dizziness through its increasing dissonance and softening of rhythmic definition. This strange blurring from reality to dream and back to reality is enforced by the musical score, which is at once a chronological development syncing the narrative sequence of events, and a meta-narrative continuum which determines the overall dynamic flow of the cartoon.

Yet this 'blurring of states' is an inherent function of musical discourse, where states are not only juxtaposed, sequenced or related to one another but also able to be evoked within and from one another via the practice of polyphony, transposition and modulation. These are primary ways in which tonality is a 'plane of the present' across which the musical subject moves. The key figure for travelling across this plane is the thumping bassoon ostinato which forms the basic building block for Dukas' concerto. It is designed as a self-regenerating form – once it has finished the only thing it can do is start again – which perfectly suggests the breeding brooms. The musical rhythm forms the base for an increasing hysteria as Mickey tries to halt the brooms' ceaseless reproduction.

The visual architecture of the castle, with all its steps and corridors, illustrates the development of the musical score: up and down and across and through. Each broom represents a musical instrument in the orchestra while the changes in perspective and space equate shifts of tonality in the music. This is combined with the visual detailing of water as the substance whose form one cannot control: it spreads everywhere, filling every space available. A peak is reached when the brooms – totally immersed in water – continue to execute the motion of emptying their buckets into the trough, which leads to the water filling the whole screen. The audiovisual text here (as the symbolising of the dynamics of music) literally and figuratively reaches saturation point; all architectural space and all musical tonality are seemingly exhausted; water is everywhere, and every modulation of the ostinato has been covered.

Dir: James Algar; **Prod:** Walt Disney, Ben Sharpsteen; **Scr:** Perce Pearce, Carl Fallberg; **Animation Supervision:** Fred Moore, Vladimir Tytla; **Sourced Score:** Paul Dukas; **Main Cast:** Mickey Mouse.

Forbidden Planet
US, 1954 – 98 mins
Fred Macleod Wilcox

Hollywood. Science fiction. 1956. Canary yellow and bright red 3-D lettering zooms forward: *Forbidden Planet*. The background is space – planetarium-style diorama space; deep blue dotted with milky swirls of stars. Granted that objects and images must be big, bright and bold, but how will they sound? They will sound . . . reverberant. As *Forbidden Planet*'s credits roll across the screen against a vast vacuum of night, its solely electronic and wholly non-musical soundtrack reverberates in echoic bleeps and tubular squawks. Such specious logic: sound of course does not operate in airless outer space as it does within earth's atmosphere. In space no one can hear your reverb.

Reverb is heavily applied to *Forbidden Planet*'s synthetic sound effects firstly to invoke the expansive opening of interplanetary frontiers, and secondly to evoke an imposing sense of size and space. At least fifteen centuries of European church architecture used reverb to conjure up thundering scale and omnipotent power; sci-fi movies followed suit with their own brand of technological mysticism and God-fearing morality. As declared by *Forbidden Planet*'s opening, the emptiness of space is assumed to sound like a big, dark, empty chamber, making the film a wonderful sign of its time: archly spooky, frighteningly empty and electronically baroque.

Equally important to *Forbidden Planet*'s aural veneer is the way it foregrounds reverberation to articulate space. Psychoacoustically, reverb grants us an out-of-body experience: we can aurally separate what we hear from the space in which it occurs. While this sensation was a wholly acoustic trait since time immemorial, the recording, rendering and representation of its texture was rediscovered as an 'electro-acoustic' feature in recorded sound. Fetishised by the pop music industry and the electro-acoustic academy alike, it stands as a prime signifier of a recording's spatialisation. No wonder an archetypal 'space movie' like *Forbidden Planet* amplifies that very texture of 'space'.

Forbidden Planet famously signposts the clumsy but charming audiovisual fusion of 'electronics' with 'sci-fi' which persists today. Apart from the overt reference to the beeping pops of radio, shortwave and radar technologies of the period, the importation of a more rarefied electronic realisation and manipulation grants *Forbidden Planet* an aural depth which matches the grandeur of its absent orchestra. The film's landmark status thus comes as much from its sophisticated soundscape as it does from sumptuous widescreen production design.

Yet beyond effect, *Forbidden Planet*'s 'score' is reigned by its narrative drive. Its production design proposes that the planet's deserts are remnants of oceanic regions, hence the film looks like an empty fish tank cluttered with hardened coralular and spongeforic formations. And just as the music score emphasises reverb where there cannot be any, so too do 'bubbly' sounds percolate incessantly, incongruously overlaying an underwater presence on a barren visual terrain. Of course, sounds heard by our ears underwater do not carry the full-frequency detail with which film music and sound portray aquatic conditions and sensations. Eventually, a mental landscape is conjured forth by these audible yet invisible presences, as they relate to the fetid subconscious of Morbius (Pidgeon), whose repressed energy controls the dynamos running deep in the bowels of the planet. In a bizarre match of geographical and psychological logic, the out-of-body experiences of reverb-in-space and aquasonics-on-land perfectly complement each other in *Forbidden Planet*'s psychic zone. The acoustics are unreal, the sound is watertight, and the symbolism is sound.

Dir: Fred Macleod Wilcox; **Prod:** Nicholas Nayfack; **Scr:** Irving Block, Allen Adler, Cyril Hume; **DOP:** George J. Folsey; **Editor:** Ferris Webster; **Score:** Louis and Bebbe Barron; **Sound:** Wesley C. Miller; **Main Cast:** Walter Pidgeon, Anne Francis, Leslie Nielsen.

Gate of Flesh (*Nikutai no mon*)
Japan, 1968 – 90 mins
Seijun Suzuki

Like a prostitute that can't wait for her session to finish so she can start another, *Gate of Flesh* commences its soundtrack before the film starts. Over the Nikkatsu logo, a barrage of machine-gun fire and air-raid sirens is blasted. No proud and glorious trumpets here, as music is decimated by the noise of war. The bombing is then cut dead by a mournful ballad played on *shimasen* as credits depicting paintings of waif-like naked women linger. Another implosive cut and we are tracking with a starving girl, Maya (Nogawa) as she wanders lost through Tokyo's 'city of beasts'. Hordes of gnarling prostitutes ravenously claw at American GIs. Playing over Maya's fretful gaze is a drinking ballad distorted through a street PA system. Sen (Kasai) spies Maya and offers her work, and asks if she has ever been with an American. The screen suddenly explodes with a billowing American flag as a *taiko* drum pounds an incessantly morbid rhythm: flash-back to Maya's body being found by a black priest after having been raped by GIs . . .

Typical of Japanese 60s 'B-grade' cinema from the post-Occupation period, *Gate of Flesh* is still at war with itself, and is self-constituted as a panic-ridden bullet-riddled audiovisual text. Bearing the violent marks of collage which typifies twentieth-century modernist representation, the film is a frighteningly colourful and euphorically spiteful construction of sounds, images, voices, colours, edits, movements, faces and bodies, hurled against each other in an explosive dance of death. Steering well away from sanctioned forms of critique, *Gate of Flesh*'s Jap-Pop Art refracts its colonised American modernity into a shattered mirror of mimicry and face-pulling without any of the camp sensibilities inlaid by American and European experiments in Pop Art.

The eponymous 'gate of flesh' is a bombed-out shell of a building controlled by Sen and her three fellow prostitutes, Miyo, O-Rok and

Gate of Flesh: forcing sound to fight with image

Omachi, plus the newly joined Maya. Their psyches and bodies form a gate of flesh – one that barricades itself from the harshness of the outside world. In their screaming psycho-sexual space, they reign, heady with the power they crave, insatiably fucking to stay alive and buy food. Their voices energise their space in an onslaught of caterwauls, screeches, songs, orgasms, cries and laughter. No walls contain them; there is no discernible inside; all is exposed. In a proto-Pop rejection of the kabuki legacy of staging, the women are not patterned into gestural relief by ornate kimonos. Instead, they each wear a single colour all the time, jarring against the dark rubble of their surroundings, never fitting in and never relating to them. At moments, their predatory nature is symbolised by a roving spotlight which renders their domain part-theatre stage, part-prison quadrangle. Sound and music behave identically, screaming, writhing and contorting at every juncture, forcing sound to fight with image with the same emotional savagery of these women of flesh, struggling to live.

Dir: Seijun Suzuki; **Prod:** Kaneo Iwai; **Scr:** Goro Tanada; **DOP:** Shigeyoshi Mine; **Editor:** Akira Suzuki; **Score:** Naozumi Yamamoto; **Sound:** Tsuguo Yoneda; **Main Cast:** Tamiko Ishii, Satoko Kasai, Kayo Matsuo, Yumiko Nogawa, Jo Shishido, Misako Tominaga.

Godzilla – King of Monsters (Kaiju o Gojira)
Japan, 1954 – 98 mins
Inoshiro Honda

Tokyo. Downtown. Peak hour. Three sonic booms are sounded: Godzilla is about to perform some radical urban redevelopment. In *Godzilla – King of Monsters*, those sonic booms function as phonemes, always introduced as an off-screen sound effect signalling the arrival of Godzilla's mighty power. Yet despite their iconic clarity, their means of production remains indistinct: somewhere between fist bangs on a metal door and mallet strikes on a timpani, recorded with slight distortion and heavy compression. Their detonation tells us we have arrived somewhere between sound, music and noise. Somewhere outside of European concert halls; somewhere on an Asian soundtrack.

You hear nothing when sumo wrestlers thump, pound and careen precariously within a minuscule space too small for their size and movement. The similarity in scale between a sumo wrestler in his ring and Godzilla in Tokyo (a man inside a rubber suit destroying a miniature diorama) suggests that *Godzilla – King of Monsters* is sumo with post-dubbed sound. In the West, the sprung mat of wrestling already acts as a live sound board – a gross, square drum that amplifies the fall of the vanquished body, giving us a sound uncannily like Godzilla's own thunderous footsteps. The Eastern silence of sumo, the Western explosiveness of American federation wrestling, and their monstrous fusion in *Godzilla – King of Monsters*; each conveys the feeling of being physically struck and racked internally by subsonic shock waves. In sumo, these waves are imagined as if your ear is on the ground; in wrestling, they are amplified by separate mic placement. In *Godzilla – King of Monsters*, they are reconstructed through tape manipulation to unnaturally suggest a terrorised timpani and grant us a hyper-tactile sonic experience.

It is this physicality that describes the fluctuations of the Eastern soundtrack, setting it in contrast to the thematic projection of thrills beamed and directed from European soundtracks. Explosiveness on Occidental soundtracks is precisely that: destructive detonations which unleash audiovisual spectacles. But like voyeurs to car crashes, we remain outside their damaging trajectory. Japan's pragmatic acceptance of earthquakes has determined a peculiarly sonic relation to the earth, tremulous and vibrational as it is despite its hardened density. When Godzilla stomps, trains derail, power plants explode, and buildings tumble; these spectacles allow a Japanese audience to relive similar environmental traumas.

Physicality also extends to the metaphorical operation of the score. On the surface a corny loping of grossly bawdy riffs, the score's atonal pantomime is not to be read as merely representing Godzilla, but as a musical evocation of a man lumbering around in a rubber suit. Presumed to be one of the most pathetic of 'rubber-suit' monster movies, *Godzilla – King of Monsters* is an ornate display of heightened artifice, wherein slo-mo photography, miniature vehicles, constructed dioramas, suspension wires, puppetry and costumery are extensions of *bunraku* puppet theatre. The score importantly acknowledges this and is aligned to it, creating a unique audiovisual mime whose spectacle generates a complex of sono-musical reverberations.

Dir: Inoshiro Honda; **Prod:** Tomoyuki Tanaka; **Scr:** Inoshiro Honda, Shigeru Kayama, Takeo Murata; **DOP:** Masao Tamai; **Editor:** Yasunobu Taira; **Score:** Akira Ifukube; **Sound:** Uchiro Minawa; **Main Cast:** Takashi Shimura, Akira Takarada, Momoko Kochi, Akihiko Hirata.

Goodfellas
US, 1990 – 146 mins
Martin Scorsese

After its gruesome prologue, *Goodfellas* holds on an extreme close-up of an eye – a bluff, as the film constructs dense aural architecture across time, charting Henry Hill's (Liotta) changing perception of himself and his social reality. Music – more precisely, its record production – creates exacting memory spaces for the unfolding of the film's scenes. The vitality and brashness of the 60s is grossly framed by the hyper-compressed reverberating rotundity of songs by the Ronettes, the Shangri-Las and Bobby Darrin; the blunted and altered perceptions of the 70s are harshly boxed by the fractured multi-tracking and denaturalised mixing of songs by Derek and the Dominos, Brewer and Shipley, and Sid Vicious.

As the film hurtles towards the present, changes in the orientation of Henry's commentary parallel changes in the apparatuses of stereo production, moving from breathy, lingering valve mics and line-fed echo chambers to overloaded effects-chaining compensating the fetishisation of acoustically 'dead' studios. *Goodfellas* deftly sutures the psychoacoustics of microphone placement into the wavering equilibrium Henry experiences through the narration of his story. Song in *Goodfellas* is a realm into which the film is imported, in reversal of the standard audiovisual hierarchy which governs much film mixing.

The voice of Henry is also 'de-literated', performing less as a crude literary device so beloved of 'personal cinema' and more as a breathing, sweaty being. Ironically, it is more like hearing someone talk from their incarceration than listening to someone read from their memoirs. Not only does Henry's voice govern space, it also controls time. All visual action – and even most musical placement – is cued and concatenated by the very phrasing of his words. At moments, the film even goes into freeze-frame, demonstrating the authorial power with which he is recalling his past. Furthermore, the voice track is a highly processed and compacted assemblage. Rhythm, banter, slang, intonation – all are edited into a sparkling meta-performance which places the voice centre stage, projecting arcs of hyperactive energy as Henry's voice conveys the effects of thinking too many things at once. This anxious shrinkage evident in both the recording and construction of Henry's vocals characterises *Goodfellas* as a compressed text in both sonic and dramatic terms.

Running perpendicular to this compression is a strangely elasticised relation between Henry's voiceover and the accompanying songs. While the songs fragrantly cast Henry's mind back to the heady time and space of his narration, their vivid placement fluctuates in its attraction to the 'present' of the film's narration. Songs set earlier lean towards the present more than they perform nostalgically to hold us in their past, as if Henry's edginess is fatally drawing us forwards despite the song's retrospective cling. Songs set later are desperately tugged back to the past – to a time prior to Henry's gradual demise. Ultimately, when he is younger, Henry is driven to move forwards; as he gets older – but not wiser – he is obsessed with delaying, holding, halting his world to prevent its collapse. How apt to close with him mocking us direct to the camera, interred invisibly in the Witness Protection Programme as we hear the orchestra slip into atonality as Sid Vicious whines 'My Way'.

Dir: Martin Scorsese; **Prod:** Irwin Winkler; **Script:** Nicholas Pileggi, Martin Scorsese; **DOP:** Michael Ballhaus; **Editor:** Thelma Schoonmaker, James Kwei; **Songs:** include Tony Bennett, the Moonglows, the Cadillacs, the Chantels, the Shangri-Las, Aretha Franklin, Bobby Darrin, Cream, Muddy Waters, Derek and the Dominos, Nilsson, Sid Vicious; **Sound Design:** Skip Lievsay; **Main Cast:** Robert De Niro, Ray Liotta, Joe Pesci, Lorraine Bracco, Paul Sorvino, Frank Sivero, Tony Darrow.

Guided Muscle
US, 1955 – 9 mins
Charles M. Jones

Play *Guided Muscle* – a Roadrunner and Coyote cartoon from the early 50s – and shut your eyes. Listen to the soundtrack: presses, plants and pumps from fantastic factories; valves, pistons, ignitions from unimagined motors; gears, exhausts and turbines from eviscerated engines. This is the true sound of the 50s orchestra: a machine of sonic production, unromanticised for its collapse of music yet fetishised for the sheer power and beauty of its metallica.

One of a number of peak Warner Bros. cartoons from the mid-40s to the mid-50s, *Guided Muscle* exemplifies how deeply the mechanical had then penetrated the popular consciousness. Outrightly labelling its psycho-sexual melt of war and sex, *Guided Muscle* joins many Warner Bros. cartoons as part of a mass medium which auditioned both the scarring cacophony of wartime trauma and the heady eroticism of post-war technologies. It has its share of pumping, thrusting, shafting dynamics – as the Roadrunner is ejaculated through space by a bow, a rubber band, a cannon – as well as more overtly sexual suggestions courtesy of giant demolition balls and the Roadrunner covered in lubricating grease.

Tightly and fastidiously synced to the sounds of rocket propulsion, propeller roar, engine rumble and turbine whine, the fusion of sexual symbolism and machine noise in *Guided Muscle* is typical of the post-war cartoon. Marketed as mere icons of wackiness today, the Coyote and Roadrunner cycle of cartoons was originally digested by audiences whose listening had been profoundly altered by bomb detonations; to whom the metallic ring of chrome appliances was titillating, and the smell of exhaust a futuristic fragrance.

Guided Muscle opens with the pretence of the Coyote ('Eatibus Almost Anythingus') cooking a tin can and serving it up to himself as a delicacy – all to the ludicrous detailing of whimsical, jazzy fragments. To the camera, he acknowledges the absurdity of this and sweeps it into a bin. On cue, the Roadrunner ('Velocitus Delectibus') suddenly rips past him in a blaze of noise, smoke and speed. The ensuing chase of the Roadrunner by the Coyote in *Guided Muscle* on the one hand can be viewed as humorous existentialism, like Beckett on speed in the desert. On the other hand, it can be seen as horrific sexuality, like Ballard on heat in the desert. The power and energy of the soundtrack's sono-musicality is certainly more an unleashing of dynamised machinic and libidinal noise than anything else in its gestural portrayal of demented pursuit and ravenous desire. The metaphoric jazz that accompanies lascivious cartoons where gender is foregrounded (like MGM's *Red Hot Riding Hood*, 1943, and *Swing Shift Cinderella*, 1945) is here eschewed for an octane-fuelled cocktail of pre- and post-war jazz populism and unadulterated noise, as gender is replaced by genetics and musicalised social ritual is replaced by orchestrated sexual bombast.

The sonic explosiveness of *Guided Muscle* can be further contextualised by its place in the entertainment of its time. Throughout the hysterically utopian 50s, noise – a gigantic sound effects library of destruction, detonation and devastation – perversely reigns on the cinematic soundtrack. Blockbusters went big on the screen, high on moral content, lurid in their visuality, and loud in their sound design. Formed entirely from the shards, frames, snaps and cracks of those blockbusters, *Guided Muscle* exploits its release from cinematography to veer towards sonic pornography.

Dir: Charles M. Jones; Scr: Michael Maltese; **Layouts:** Philip DeGuard; **Animation:** Richard Thompson, Ken Harris, Ben Washman, Abe Levitow; **Score:** Carl Stalling; **Sound Effects:** Tregg Brown; **Cast:** Coyote, Roadrunner.

Gummo
US, 1997 – 95 mins
Harmony Korine

Just as one must listen to someone in order to understand them, *Gummo* presents a cinematic mirror which audiovisually throws back to us our collective inability to listen to those presumed problematic: kids.

Gummo ventures into the territory of dysfunctionality further than most would like. The film is intermittently narrated by Tummler (Sutton) who, in a series of near-incomprehensible confessions, revelations and delusions, cautiously guides us through his hometown in Kentucky. Its Midwestern outer-suburban dead-end world of nowhere is literally upside down, referenced as such by Tummler's vague assertion that the area's only claim to fame is that a huge tornado swept through there some years back. Sound- and image-tracks are strewn like debris around his mumbling. Saturated home-video grain, blurred Polaroids and erotic 35mm close-ups hover around their subjects, obsessively lingering on their skin, hair, lips. Actors, non-actors, wannabes and nobodies are chaotically integrated to generate measures of controlled and uncontrolled interaction. Dialogue is so ridden with vernacular, vulgarity and virulence that it builds an impenetrable wall in contrast to the excessive and discomforting voyeurism which impels the film's camera work. Music is repellently inappropriate, desultorily matched or virtually allergic to the film's images rather than merely counterpointing them.

An anti-matter version of *The Beverly Hillbillies*, *Gummo* is an entirely unwelcoming film about the disenfranchised who are seldom welcomed anywhere, and whose mode of address to the viewer/auditor is likely to repel, revoke and repulse. No noble sprits of the little people here; no music to accord them respect. And that's the power of *Gummo*: its unflinching cinematic face-to-face with the brethren from American tabloid TV (a large portion are non-actors documented and collaged into

(Next page) Gummo: sound and music at the border of self-destruction

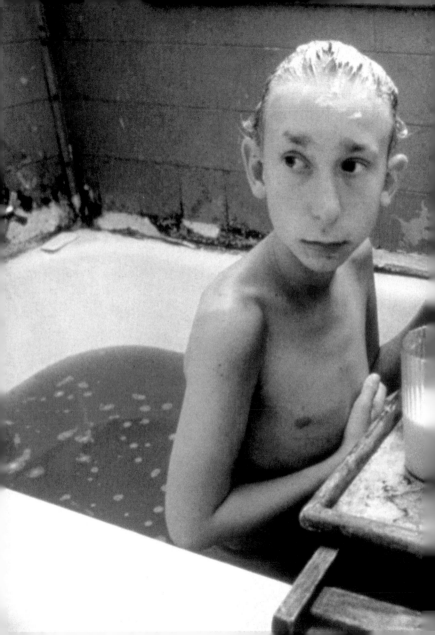

the film), as if they have been blown into the cinema by some apocalyptic hurricane. The song selection's 'appropriateness' is thus coded with the unfitting quality of its subjects. Crackling vinyl of yodelling accompanies Bunny Boy (Sewell) as he spits from an overpass onto traffic going somewhere; gruff metal grunge rises in thick dark waves as Tummler and Solomon (Reynolds) ride their bikes downhill to nowhere; Buddy Holly's 'Every Day' twinkles as Bunny Boy takes turns in kissing Dot (Sevigny) and Helen (Carisa Glucksman) as they swim in a dirty backyard pool in the rain. Yet these moments of music become unexpectedly poetic through their widening of the scopic fix the film has on its subjects.

Elsewhere, music is disallowed by the weird and unrecognisable rumbles of distortion which place the film at the border of self-destruction. Sounding somewhere between the impossibly amplified hiss and noise on a police interrogation Dictaphone and the wall-of-noise from a local news station's live broadcast at the site of some massive devastation, *Gummo*'s sound design welcomes the sonically rejected as openly as the film's inhabitants allow us into their kitchen on Saturday night as they get drunk and violently destroy their furniture in impotent rage.

Dir: Harmony Korine; **Prod:** Cary Woods; **Scr:** Harmony Korine; **DOP:** Jean-Yves Escoffier; **Editor:** Christopher Tellefsen; **Songs:** Buddy Holly, Nifelheim, Absu, Eyehategod, Electric Hellfire Club, Bethlehem, Burzum, Bathory, Namanax, Mortician, Mystifier, Destroy All Monsters; **Sound Design:** Steve Borne; **Main Cast:** Jacob Sewell, Nick Sutton, Jacob Reynolds, Chloë Sevigny.

Hail Mary (Je vous salue, Marie)
France, 1985 – 107 mins
Jean-Luc Godard

Hail Mary is a cinematic Russian doll. Comprised of two films (*The Book of Mary* and *Je vous salue, Marie*), it proceeds by a series of self-divisions and self-enclosures, splitting into microcosms whose detail and significance span ever outwards. Thematically, the mystery of conception horizontally connects both films, while the second major film vertically delves into the macrocosmological corridors opened by its reworking of the New Testament. Once there, a fractal matrix comprised of audiovisual threads works as a net to illustrate the means by which it has arrived at its version of the birth of Jesus.

From a theological perspective, the overwhelming impenetrability of *Hail Mary* accords the Bible and its mysteries appropriate depth; the film's narrative choice is to not reduce the biblical text to mere plot and casual action. The film appears to be centred on the dysfunctional relationship between young Marie (Roussel) and petrol-station attendant Joseph (Rode) and his doubting of her unaccountable pregnancy, but a parallel story intersects. We are spliced into a scenario of a professor (Johan Leysen) taking his students on a field excursion and developing a slight affair with one of his students (Anne Gautier). The disorienting switching between these two stories appears random until one perceives how the sound from one is joined to the image of the other, playing out a series of syncretic variations which fuse the two symbolically, thematically and philosophically.

Images of bulbous fertility – the moon, water, fruit, Marie's abdomen – are conjoined by sounds of penetration – rocks disturbing the smooth water, slivers of string quartet harmonies, car horns, door knocks. In a meta-sexual sense, sound mates with image. This is the audiovisual means by which Nature is posited as a holistic sonorum whose eventfulness is determined by a series of balances and flows. The moon is linked to the tides, which are linked to menstrual cycles, which are linked to moments of conception. Crickets, bees, insects, birds often create slabs, walls and curtains of atmosphere, edited into rhythmic occurrences across image sequences. Passages of wind are called up whenever a semi-mystical moment occurs, referencing the visitation of the Archangel Gabriel (Lacoste) breathing life into Mary for her Immaculate Conception. Planes, helicopters and traffic are woven as strange lines and curves into the networking between the contracting spaces of Joseph and Mary's dissolution and the expanding spaces as the professor pushes his students into deeper cosmological inquiry.

Hail Mary becomes a crystalline text of biblical interpretation when one reads the cartography of its soundtrack. Each sonic incident – one of rupture, erasure, collision or counterpoint – is a signpost to an image, moment or scene elsewhere in the story. These sonic expulsions delineate the matricular structure of *Hail Mary* – one that violently discounts linearity, causality and symbolism, and in place offers laterality, simultaneity and iconography. Through openly querying whose authorial voice speaks in the Bible, *Hail Mary* comes to regard the Bible as a utilitarian template that simply occurred (as the intertitle joining the two films states) 'at that time'. One is then able to draw long-reaching and wide-ranging associations between the film's narrative and whichever events one chooses to align with it. Echoing this complete inversion of the precepts of fundamentalism, *Hail Mary* presents a total audiovisual inversion of cinema.

Dir: Jean-Luc Godard; **Prod:** uncredited; **Scr:** Jean-Luc Godard; **DOP:** Jacques Firmann, Jean-Bernard Menoud; **Editor:** Anne-Marie Miéville; **Sourced Score:** Johann Sebastian Bach, John Coltrane, Antonín Dvořják; **Sound Design:** Francois Musy; **Main Cast:** Myriem Roussel, Thierry Rode, Philippe Lacoste, Manon Andersen, Jara Kohan.

The Haunting
US, 1999 – 113 mins
Jan De Bont

Spooky movies about haunted mansions invariably highlight insignificant sounds to terrorise the audience, scaring us with a sudden door creak or an unexpected window rattle. If we were suddenly made aware of all the tones and tunings which comprise the residua of our everyday activities, we would find our tremulous homes as terrifying as Hill House in *The Haunting*. Here is another nightmarishly over-designed special-effects movie, but its use of sound amplifies how much we presume insignificant in acoustic auras. For as baroque as the visual design in the film is, its ocular loudness is no match for the way the sound design forces itself upon our ears.

An early moment in *The Haunting* touches this taut gauze stretched between sound and image. Eleanor (Taylor) is wakened by three soft off-screen thumps, which she dozily presumes to be her recently departed ill mother banging the wall for aid. Three more bangs, which we audit as unreal and unearthly. Then three more bangs which shake the cinema auditorium near to the point of collapse: both Eleanor and we know something exists beyond the sonic. Those three layers of big bangs illustrate three levels of aural consciousness: the displaced referential (all the sound we don't listen to); the forced ethereal (that same corpus of sound rendered noticeable); and the inverted inescapable (the realisation that we might not be able ever to unlisten to sound). Illogically vacillating between a fear of silence and a dread of deafness: that is truly spooky.

When the evil Hugh Crain first marks his possessive presence, the off-screen pounding actually rattles the light fittings and air-conditioning ducts of the cinema. This hyper-fantastic aesthetic to the sound design is ultimately ironic, in that on numerous occasions, characters in the film query each other – 'Didn't you hear that noise?' – about sounds that

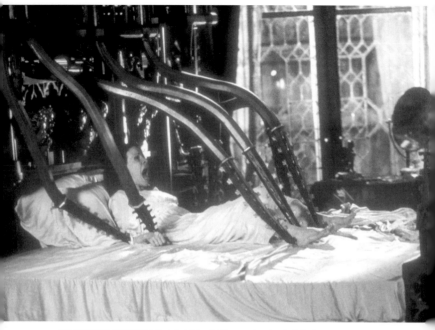

The Haunting: vacillating between a fear of silence and a dread of deafness

occurred at deafening decibels in the very next room. All plausibility fades because the sonic purpose of the film is not to describe a reality or portray a psychological state, but to unnerve the audience: to go beyond the screen and into us.

More importantly, the complexity by which a film these days must achieve such results has little to do with earlier constructs and paradigms of sound design based on drastic binaries of silence/noise. Film sound – not unlike rarefied musical performances – expects that an audience can disengage from the noise of their environment and 'become silent' for the duration of the film. But 'silence' is becoming an increasingly doubted concept, let alone ideal. In a contemporary acoustic climate, where the droning pink noise of air conditioners and computer hard drives colours the world a fleshy tone of heaving ambience, the on/off tricks of sound editing fast lose their emotional power in the cinematic realm. As mainstream entertainment, *The Haunting* signposts the paths to be taken in order to reinvest the cinema with the power to psychoacoustically make us cogniscent of the delightful terror to be found in everyday sound.

Dir: Jan De Bont; **Prod:** Susan Arnold, Donna Roth, Colin Wilson; **Scr:** David Self; **DOP:** Karl Walter Lindenlaub; **Editor:** Michael Kahn; **Score:** Jerry Goldsmith; **Sound Design:** Gary Rydstrom, Frank E. Eulner, Ethan Van der Ryn; **Main Cast:** Lili Taylor, Liam Neeson, Catherine Zeta-Jones, Owen Wilson, Bruce Dern, Marian Seldes.

Heat
US, 1995 – 164 mins
Michael Mann

The blurred mix of selected songs and composed score in *Heat* creates a tonal web from which a meta-score is discernible, based on externalising pre-recorded songs to extrapolate and extemporise their recordings into the expanded audiovisual design of the film. *Heat* seeks to narrate, compile and underscore through song, to arrive in parts at a 'song-seeming score' which exploits the dynamics, characteristics and idiosyncrasies of pop/rock recordings. In place of the blunt appropriation and importation which typifies the often reviled use of pop songs in movies, *Heat* extenuates a song's sonic traits to define the material realm of a scene. Combining a calming and contiguous track selection with a melting, amorphous score (for two drum kits, twin basses, string quartet and six electric guitars), the film plays sophisticated games in breaking down all distinction between song and score while building upon the armoury of effects and figures generated within song recording rather than film scoring.

   Heat's leaning towards ambient styling is less to do with a vague contemporaneity and lazy self-effacement, and more to do with a synchronicity between the de-rhythmatised harmonic splaying of songs by Eno, Passengers, Moby, Kronos Quartet, Terje Rypdal, Michael Brook, Einsturzende Neubauten and Lisa Gerrard, and the exhausted, emotional drainage of Vincent Hanna (Pacino) and Neal McCauley (De Niro), whose sense of purposeful conflict is rendered meaningless by the film's conclusion. The ambient brethren of *Heat*'s soundtrack is crucial to the creeping existentialism which eventually upturns the film's epic form. And just as the sound of space has become the prime erogenous zone of ambient music, *Heat*'s musical scoring is the prime means of actively spatialising the film's locations and environments – especially as a counterpoint to the highly fragmented framing aesthetic employed by the cinematography.

From the horripilant softness of the low-level string murmuring as Neal placidly takes a series of escalators in the film's opening, to the hammering synth pops and concatenated reverb bangs which crackle under the screams of employees and customers during the bank heist, ambience is actually foregrounded as style and form in *Heat*. The effect is impossible not to perceive: while many films feverishly over-score and force audiences to consume the music as vapid background slop, *Heat* highlights, amplifies and pinpoints its many delicate gestures and restrained palettes, generating a harmonic humidity which hangs thick in the air.

Yet this arises not from the music alone; *Heat* is not the result of music driving the narrative in video-clip mode. The stoic stature and impassive demeanour of the gang – including Chris (Kilmer), Michael (Tom Sizemore) and Nate (Voight) – coalesce into a rock-hard monumental troupe. Their extreme suppression of reaction and the steeled nerves which control their actions cast them in frozen relief, often in craggy close-ups. Against their facial fortresses, a veil of musical ambience is thrown; it racks their emotional walls with a resounding echo that carries throughout the film.

Dir: Michael Mann; **Prod:** Art Linson, Michael Mann; **Scr:** Michael Mann; **DOP:** Dante Spinotti; **Editor:** Pasquale Buba, William Goldenberg, Dov Hoenig, Tom Rolf; **Score:** Elliot Goldenthal; **Sourced Songs:** Passengers, Einsturzende Neubauten, Moby, Brian Eno, Michael Brook, Terje Rypdal, Lisa Gerrard; **Supervising Sound Editor:** Per Hallberg, Larry Kemp; **Main Cast:** Al Pacino, Robert De Niro, Val Kilmer, Jon Voight.

Hour of the Wolf (*Vargtimmen*)
Sweden, 1968 – 88 mins
Ingmar Bergman

As if the film is building its sets and rigging its lights, *Hour of the Wolf*'s opening credits roll over the unseen sound of a film set being readied. An unseen voice calls out, 'Camera – action'. But then this sonic deus ex machina opens onto a cabin atop a remote Swedish island. A woman walks out and speaks to us, explaining that we have her departed husband's diary; everything is in there. *Hour of the Wolf* is that diary presented in cinematic form, its words silenced through the film's sounds and images. Documenting the repressed and unrepressed violence within artist Johan (von Sydow), it flashes forwards and backwards in surges and ellipses, juxtaposing his early calmer moments with the later depths of his despair.

Presumed to be an idyllic spot for Johan and Alma (Ullmann), the island becomes a shrinking prison for Johan, as his chauvinistic verve withers in proportion to the self-exposure of his seething neuroses. Racked with pain inflicted by his inner demons, he ruptures the silence of their household continually. When he shows Alma some of his drawings, he noisily flips each page, scaring her with the monstrous visions he keeps inside. He further unsettles her by noting the passing of a minute – barking the passages in ten-second blocks. The naturalistic quiet of the house is easily disturbed by the sounds of his movement, transforming it into an uncomfortable realm for Alma, just as his self-loathing discomforts him.

This is in contrast to the heightened and stylised passages which envelop both Johan and Alma when they encounter the decadent Von Merkens and their friends ensconced in a cavernous mansion. The voices, faces and presences of these social monstrosities – fuel for Johan's growing delusional paranoia and his most nightmarish sketches – are depicted as encroaching, interrupting and deafening. Their decrepit chatter suffocates Johan and Alma, silencing the artist and his wife. A demonic aspect particularly taints Lindhorst (Rydeberg) when he puts on a puppet play to a movement from *The Magic Flute*, which – in Alma's mind – appears to be staged by living homunculi. Each time Johan returns there, the mansion's labyrinth of corridors and chambers transforms its interior into an audiovisual hell.

Music announces itself a full hour into the film. By this stage, Alma has read his diary and Johan is living a duality of rational observation and morbid behaviour. The music reflects the heavily pregnant knowing which now pervades their house as Johan opens up to Alma in the middle of the night – the 'hour of the wolf' when most old people pass away – and tells her of more unsettling incidents from his past. The most tormenting is his recollection of having irrationally killed a young boy by the ocean. The score throughout this scene is chilling – all the more so due to the erasure of sound bar the boy's screams. Flutes scrape like brakes, trumpets buzz like hornets, clarinets tear like nails: dead centre and ground zero of Johan's maddening din. From this black hole of discord, Johan will not return.

Dir: Ingmar Bergman; **Prod:** Lars-Owe Carlberg; **Script:** Ingmar Bergman; **DOP:** Sven Nykvist; **Editor:** Ulla Ryghe; **Score:** Lars Johan Werle; **Sound Editor:** Evald Andersson, Lennart Engholm; **Sound Recording:** Per-Olof Pettersson; **Main Cast:** Max von Sydow, Liv Ullmann, Gertrud Fridh, Georg Rydeberg, Erland Josephson, Ingrid Thulin.

House by the River
US, 1950 – 88 mins
Fritz Lang

In the American neo-Gothic world of *House by the River*, the ornate
rules. Brooches, brocade, bustles and balustrades drape people and
objects like a suffocating shroud. Lit somewhere between an
expressionist stage and a noir location, the film doesn't merely narrate: it
snares its characters, slowly sinking them into a murderous mire as
novelist Stephen Byrne (Hayward) strangles his servant Emily (Patrick)
and lures his brother John (Bowman) into dumping her body in the river
adjoining Stephen's house.

Inordinately early in the film, Stephen is turned on by a series of
triggers which prime him for his journey into Gothic sexuality. From
outside his house, Stephen notices Emily turn on the light in the upstairs
bathroom. The score blasts its labelling of this first trigger. As Stephen
approaches the house, music is quelled as Emily drains her bath. Stephen
listens to the drain, 'seeing' the water run down the pipes as he 'sees'
Emily's body dripping wet. The gurgling on the soundtrack is vulgar and
verges on being sonically pornographic. Stephen moves inside in silence,
drinks some wine, then douses the light as Emily's silhouette appears on
the landing. Hidden in the enveloping blackness of the house, his arousal
peaks as Emily's disembodied thighs carve through the long vaginal slit of
her gown, her slippered feet creaking the stairs with rounded tones as
she descends. Now a completely surreal attractor, she unknowingly
enters the house's transformative domain of unrepressed lust. No musical
accompaniment whatsoever; silence signifies the erasure of the human
and the amplification of its Other.

The score gathers in lurid folds around the brooding psychosis of
Stephen, portraying his complete lack of remorse and his increasingly
aroused state as he fictionalises his escapades, while the police attempt
to solve the murder once Emily's body is discovered. The music's
uncontrolled flirtatiousness is fixed on Stephen's psycho-sexual

House by the River: silence signifying the erasure of the human

awakening, typifying him as a cruelly modern sex criminal despite the film's turn-of-the-century setting. When Stephen sees that the tides have raised Emily's body from the depths of the river, he sets out at night to recover it. Half-desperate and half-thrilled, he scans the water, imagining her waving hair in the reeds floating from the river banks. The music responds with swirling clarinets, connoting the sleazy ambience of a stripper's dance.

As score and sets aim an audiovisual spotlight on the interior make-up of Stephen's sexuality, *House by the River* reveals itself to be less an expressionist decoration and more a surrealist evocation. Its fixation on the sexually charged aura of objects, surfaces, textures and sounds creates a web of paraphiliac hot-spots which trigger Stephen, awakening him to his most repressed and unsavoury desires. The Gothic environment is thus the dormant miasma of urges waiting to brush up against the house's velvet corridors. With dank poetic justice, the film concludes abruptly when Stephen perceives the ghost of Emily melting out of a flowing curtain, which wraps itself around him and leads to his demise. Lost in his own neurosis, he is swallowed up by the house's own darkness.

Dir: Fritz Lang; **Prod:** Howard Welsch; **Scr:** Mel Dinelli; **DOP:** Edward Cronjager; **Editor:** Arthur Hilton; **Score:** George Antheil; **Sound:** Dick Tyler Sr, Howard Wilson; **Main Cast:** Louis Hayward, Jane Wyatt, Lee Bowman, Dorothy Patrick.

India Song
France, 1975 – 120 mins
Marguerite Duras

As an orange orb sets into a blue-grey azure of some temperate dusk, a young Laotian girl sings unaccompanied and unsubtitled, the beauty of her voice expressed through its isolation and incomprehension. Seeming to have heard this song, two unseen French women discuss a twelve-year-old Laotian girl who on her way to Bengal asks for directions . . . to get lost. *India Song* is identically lost, deliberately so within its labyrinth of desire, memory, repression and disassociation.

The film's detached dialogue follows the form of memory prompts, shared experiences and joint suppositions as the two women languorously sift through a faceted glass bowl of recollections. A passive voice queries that which might be in front of her; an authoritative voice undercuts all overt assumption with subtextual import. This rhythm is sustained throughout *India Song*; other voices come near and far – some unsubtitled – yet all remain on the periphery of the film's slant to the Ganges in Calcutta and the Mekong in Savannakhet. The rivers' shared flowing grandeur and tropical heat generate the stilling state of mind which these places appear to have induced in the two women.

Claimed as being set in a French embassy in India, though actually disinterred in a decaying and ornate turn-of-the-century mansion, we assume that the people parading past us constitute the French Vice Counsellor (Lonsdale), the mysterious Anne Marie Stretter (Seyrig), plus ancillary ambassadors, diplomats, delegates, their wives and associates. Furniture, fittings, fabric and fashions are traced by the camera's slow gaze; wall-sized mirrors grant us complete and uninterrupted sight of all who hover in front of them. But it is soon evident we will not be seeing a single person's lips match any voice we hear. The programme of *India Song* is thus erected at the gulf between voice and description, text and event, sound and image. Two major considerations arise from this audacious audiovisual experiment.

India Song: the gulf between voice and description

Firstly, the film's colonial background creates a 'refluxive' dislocation wherein the diplomats become emotionally disenfranchised in lands where their presence is unwanted. Trapped in mausoleums of bureaucracy, the diplomats fade into ghosts and zombies, aimlessly wandering within the confines of their power, playing out their mannered functions and social graces. Secondly, character becomes less an issue of statement and more a matter of query. Traits, motivation, impulse, background – all are erased from those we see. Their mannered posture, expired repose and roving circulation renders them empty and primed for anything. Devoid of direct response to each other, they become 'infused' with reaction: steeped in the possibility that they are relating to someone or something, but never proving it on screen.

Eroticism hangs like humidity in the air, but of a specifically bisexual and polyamorous aspect. Social coding seems to have melted away in the heat of a contagious nymphomania; these cultured dignitaries in formal attire seem to be hovering in each other's pheromonal fields more than they are consciously attracted to each other. 'I love you to the point of not seeing nor hearing.' So declares a woman's disembodied voice. In this way – dispassionately so – *India Song* can be read as a love story of the most fractured kind.

Dir: Marguerite Duras; **Prod:** Stéphane Tchalgadjieff; **Scr:** Marguerite Duras; **DOP:** Bruno Nuytten; **Editor:** Solange Leprince; **Score:** Carlos d' Alessio; **Sound:** Michel Vionnet; **Main Cast:** Delphine Seyrig, Michael Lonsdale, Claude Mann, Mathieu Carrière.

The Innocents
UK, 1961 – 100 mins
Jack Clayton

The haunting title sequence to *The Innocents* is a stilling symbiosis of
sound and image which governs the wispy unfurling of the film's ghost
story. Following a full black screen through which we discern light bird
chatter, Miss Giddens' (Kerr) distinctive features sculpt white shapes in
the void as she silently mouths prayers, her face tense and focused,
betraying a quiet desperation. Over this skeletal exposure of quietude
and privacy, a sole child's voice plaintively sings; detached, unemotional,
yet pure.

Miss Giddens' desperation is partially defined by the pernickety
nature of this typical nineteenth-century nanny, but mostly it forecasts
the impassioned attachment she holds for her new charges: young Miles
(Stephens) and his sister Flora (Franklin). She relocates to the imposing
mansion which the children call home but which she finds to be a dark
psychological maze. As she gradually discovers, the children have
befriended the ghost of Peter Quint (Wyngarde), who has killed his lover,
the previous nanny Miss Jessel (Clytie Jessop). The Gothic mansion is an
architecsonic chamber of echoes which blur the living with the dead, the
sexual with the morbid, the vocal with the possessed. Miss Giddens' own
breathless praying mingles with the soft sobbing of Miss Jessel and the
excitedly hushed gossiping of Miles and Flora. Miss Giddens ventures
through the mansion time and again to locate the origin of a detached
laugh, a lost cry, a chilling breath.

The child's melody over the opening title is found to be sung by
Flora; the song is a melancholic refrain originally sung by Miss Jessel, but
which is now spiritually interred in the innocent vocals of Flora. Miles
similarly uses a haunting two-note call when searching for Flora, imbuing
it with a sexual desire due to Quint's predatory roost within Miles'
innocent being. Eventually, the bond between Quint and Miss Jessel is
replicated in an unsettling attunement between Miles and Flora. Their

presence within the mansion shifts from lost children crying for release to blackened souls trapped in a sexual purgatory. Sound within and without the mansion reflects and enhances the moments of their possession and the degree to which their vessels amplify the wandering lust of the ghosts of Quint and Miss Jessel.

Sometimes Miss Giddens' intuits these ethereal occurrences of transgression and usurpation; other times she is suddenly conscious of transformative incidents around her. At these latter moments, she will suddenly be wrought from her acoustic space and jettisoned into an alternative synchronous dimension where time and space appear corrupted. There, deep hums, wind draughts, flapping pigeons and temperate breaths catch the back of her neck, generating a cinesonic horripilation that marks *The Innocents* as a chilling film. At other moments, the film's score will deliberately halt or be struck dead in an overtly self-reflexive way, signifying the ectoplasmic manner in which the spiritual affects the material at its entrance. In these gripping silences – the most unsettling being the sudden mirage of Miss Jessel standing in the shallow lake – the terror of Miss Giddens' realisation of the ghostly realm despite her Christian denial of the supernatural unsettles her world and the soundtrack deeply.

Dir: Jack Clayton; **Prod:** Jack Clayton; **Scr:** William Archibald, Truman Capote, John Mortimer; **DOP:** Freddie Francis; **Editor:** James B. Clark; **Score:** Georges Auric; **Additional Score:** Daphne Oram; **Sound:** A. G. Ambler, Peter Musgrave, Ken Ritchie; **Main Cast:** Deborah Kerr, Peter Wyngarde, Megs Jenkins, Martin Stephens, Pamela Franklin.

The Insect Woman (*Nippon konchuki*)
Japan, 1963 – 123 mins
Shoei Imamura

Parallel to Japan's industrial rise, electronics revolution and urban rebirthing (peaking at the 1964 Tokyo Olympics), its entertainment and recording industries went into overdrive. Subliminally affected by Tokyo's overload of broadcast communications, Japan's electric boom in the 60s was the socio-industrial construct of what futurists and experimentalists had been poetically imagining for over fifty years. In a mix of semi-documentary, semi-experimental form that reflects this era, *The Insect Woman* records and notates the collapse of sound, noise and music into each other, and in doing so captures and renders the aural dissolve between all levels of sonic and musical signification.

Amorally observing and trailing the unending exploitation of Tome (Hidari), the film moves from the 1910s through to the 60s charting and annotating her episodic trauma, misfortune and degradation. With great clarity, both cinematography and sound design empty the film of historical settings and transformations and, in their place, background and off-screen sounds create a sonic web for Tome's entrapment. She is like a hardened beetle whose meandering traverses the harshest terrain; her emotional rigidity in the face of the debilitating changes which befall her arises from her brutish will to survive. Sounds of social, economic, rural, industrial and economic discourse swirl around her, from the rattling of weaving machines at the mill into which she was sold, to the caterwauling of massed prostitutes in the geisha house she joins, to the indifferent broadcast of radio and taped announcements throughout the hospital where she recovers from childbirth.

No calm is allowed on the soundtrack, just as no respite is afforded Tome, despite her exhaustion across fifty years of endurance. As the film jump-cuts years at a time and drops into disquieting freeze-frames accompanied by disconnected voiceover, sound in *The Insect Woman* encapsulates the din of life and the noise of its ruthless enterprise.

Silence never welcomes Tome as she is always surrounded, controlled and thwarted by others. The psychoacoustic effect of this is noticeable: one is worn down by the soundtrack's ceaseless and indifferent waves of aural activity. The score interpolates these waves with billows of disenfranchised orchestration – low swirling oboes, randomised jaw-harp plucks, awkward marimba plunks, assorted percussive pops, deep drum tams, dissonant violin whines – and gradually illustrates the emotional complexity born of Tome's own nomadic and aleatory route. Roaming across an unforgiving landscape and its unremitting soundscape, her inhumanity is suitably expressed by the unstoppable scurrying of an insect.

Dir: Shoei Imamura; **Prod:** uncredited; **Scr:** Keiji Hasebe, Shohei Imamura; **DOP:** Masaku Himeda; **Editor:** Matsuo Tanji; **Score:** Toshiro Mayazumi; **Sound:** uncredited; **Main Cast:** Emiko Aizawa, Masumi Harukawa, Sachiko Hidari, Emiko Higashi, Daizaburo Hirata.

I Spit on Your Grave (*Day of the Woman*)
US, 1978 – 100 mins
Mier Zarchi

Originally and tellingly titled *Day of the Woman*, *I Spit on Your Grave*
places woman on centre stage and amplifies in equal proportion her
aspiration (thirty minutes), her anguish (thirty minutes) and her abysm
(thirty minutes). Counter to the congested urban backdrop to most
rape/revenge movies, the 'stage' for Jennifer (Keaton) is Nature:
beautiful, serene, peaceful, calming. And in place of the usual wall of city
noise is the silence that accompanies the clean country air. Likewise, we
notice the emptiness of the soundtrack. Jennifer is somewhat detached
from her surroundings, and this psycho-spatial aspect of her habitation is
reflected in the quietness with which she simultaneously moves through
Nature and graces the soundtrack.

Noticeably, the expanse of 'Nature' in *I Spit on Your Grave* is non-
reverberant. Everywhere space is uncontained, rolling, continual; the
outside is consequently incapable of trapping sound, of corralling it or
bouncing it around. Whereas reverberant tunnels, corridors and halls can
intimidate due to the feeling of intrusion generated by the creepy sound
of one's footsteps, open landscapes can make one feel less self-conscious
of one's presence due to the absence of sounds which rupture the
acoustic space. This psychoacoustic phenomenon of the open landscape
typically creates a sense of ease and freedom to which Jennifer responds
positively and innocently.

Shortly after her arrival at her riverside cabin, Jennifer swims naked in
the river. The river welcomes her, folding her into its undulations and
shifting contours. There she exists free of gravity, hovering in the water's
aqueous ethereality. Jennifer's relation to her surroundings is a symbolic
act of aural sublimation. Both music and sound attain the dimensional
symbolic state of water: their presence may be perceived as a silent
airborne phenomenon, but their movement is described through waves,
flow, frequency, volume – all terms of liquidity. Through identifying with

the river and its life-flow, Jennifer profoundly takes on the characteristics of sound itself. Not merely 'at one with Nature', she sounds herself through a tactile relationship with all she touches. She strokes the water as if conducting music; she breathes air as if drinking silence; she rocks on a hammock as if recording a breeze.

No score accompanies the unobtrusive wide shots which govern the bulk of the film. Just as Jennifer moves through her space (both pre and post her traumatic raping), so are we left to observe and audit her predicament from a strained distance – textually divorced through the total erasure of music, the complete embrace of silence and the strident employment of long wide shots, yet socially implicated by experiencing the movie. Most other films would avert the gaping holes, uncomfortable pauses and painfully long passages caused by this refusal to nurture character identification. *I Spit on Your Grave* is not the by-product of such comfortable enlightenment: it is a deliberately disquieting dive into the compacted molecular grain of the cinematic scream.

Dir: Mier Zarchi; **Prod:** Mier Zarchi, Joseph Zbeda; **Scr:** Meir Zarchi; **DOP:** Yuri Haviv; **Editor:** Meir Zarchi; **Sound Effects Editor:** Alex Pfau; **Main Cast:** Camille Keaton, Eron Tabor, Richard Pace, Anthony Nichols, Gunter Kleemann.

I Stand Alone (*Seul contra tous*)
France, 1998 – 93 mins
Gaspar Noé

I Stand Alone has existential angst carved into its textuality, but its audiovisual *nous* saves it from being a protracted exercise in stylish bleakness. The film exudes a stagnant aura of inertia: unsited voiceover narration spits across numerous still images of violently ugly and banal domestic environs, creating an intense claustrophobia as we remain trapped in the Euro-macho head of the fifty-year-old Butcher (Nahon), fucked over by life, clinging to his limp cock with one hand and French patriotism with the other. Little moves on the grainy pornographic screen – especially Nahon's eyes which resemble those of a fish in the supermarket freezer – but the soundtrack energises and even terrifies the blank world depicted. Music appears at the beginning and the close of the film like mouldy red velvet curtains as some Pachelbel is played by a dying brass band. Elsewhere, a single orchestral note is struck sparsely – maybe ten times; no other music occurs. Yet repeatedly, the loud sound of a compressed, fat gunshot is synced to sudden lurches in the speed shifts exacted by digital editing.

These sonic moments initially appear gratuitous, recalling the in-your-face basketball pounds of late 80s and early 90s Nike, Pepsi or Gatorade ads. What becomes apparent is the tension created in the spaces between these highly stylised pows which violently rupture the polished naturalism of *I Stand Alone*'s murky photographic grain: before long, one is psychoacoustically primed to anticipate a bang, or to actually witness rather than audit a horrific act (which you will in the film's final fifteen minutes). True to this logic, when the pounds occur while on-screen violence is most manifest, the mix pushes the gunshot effects into the background; the vision becomes deafening. Just as an extreme tension is maintained by opposing non-natural sound design to naturalistic visuals and performances, so too does a consonant tension hum throughout the film, representing the sexual and emotional constipation of the Butcher's psychopathic disposition. In fact at the film's climax, an audible vocal humming rains uncontrollably from his mouth, as if he is trying to block out the chorus of aberrant voices which articulate his turmoil as he falls prey to the ultimate transgression of incest.

The sonic punches that periodically and perniciously drill holes into *I Stand Alone*'s soundtrack function as shocks which gradually destabilise the Butcher's head-set. The film's gunshots are not merely sonic icons of violence, but a string of detonations which reduce social conditioning to the state of post-war rubble – the definitive picture of the modern European landscape. With all psycho-familial architecture blown apart, this fifty-year-old loser stands alone as a repositioned self, ready to act out his own socially transgressive narrative. This is the male core of so much Euro angst: dumb, blank, unforgiving, unremitting. Not liberated but unleashed; not resolved but evoked. A common social being, traumatised by shocks as symbolised by the soundtrack's percussive violence, yet revealed as an unavoidably natural and dramatically inevitable figure – like the bare location sound of a street at the outer ring of Paris' industrial zones which closes the film. No operatic catharsis glorifies *I Stand Alone*; merely the respite from noise which hollows out the head of the psychologically scarred and the socially dispossessed.

Dir: Gaspar Noé; **Prod:** Lucile Hadzihalilovic, Gaspar Noé; **Scr:** Gaspar Noé; **DOP:** Dominique Colin; **Editor:** Lucile Hadzihalilovic, Gaspar Noé; **Sourced Score:** Johann Pachelbel; **Sound:** Valérie Deloof, Olivier Dô Hùu, Olivier Le Vacon; **Main Cast:** Philippe Nahon, Blandine Lenoir.

Kaidan (*Kwaidan*)
Japan, 1964 – 161 mins
Masaki Kobayashi

The radical score for *Kaidan* is arguably devoid of Western sensibilities. This omnibus ghost film, based on infamous tales from Japanese lore, has highly articulate performances and decorous staging which link it superficially to kabuki's stylised strained mimeticism. Yet its soundtrack dissolves from traditional accompaniment to a stretched, contorted and elongated grasp of the film's dark emotional trajectories. A ruthless asynchronism and flagrant disavowal of musical signification render its status as soundtrack problematic – disturbing, even.

In the first story of the anthology – *The Reconciliation (Black Hair)* – a husband (Mikuni) returns home having left his wife (Aratama) years ago. He sleeps with her ghost (she passed away unbeknown to him), then wakes to find the house in a state of total decay. Charging around the house, he crashes through the torn paper walls and rotting wood frames, and gradually withers to a skeletal corpse. Initially framed by harsh *shakuhachi* screams, the flute's raspy breathiness devolves into a score primarily comprised of improvised wood creaks. As the husband's body dries up to a skeleton, so does the score texturally contract to a fractal network of wood splinters, bone fractures and gravel sprinklings. In a bizarrely concocted imagining of Japanese sixteenth-century futurism, the 'music' sounds like an instrument being destroyed before our very ears. Furthermore, the main movement of this improvisation occurs with absolutely no synchronous sound. It takes a while to realise that what one thinks is out-of-sync sound is actually the score. The effect is haunting, memorable and exact.

In another story – *The Woman in the Snow* – a woodcutter (Nakadai) is granted a second chance after seeing Yuki, a gorgeous ghost (Kishi), kill his fellow woodcutter. While the austere, minimal *shakuhachi* tones evoke an identifiable 'Eastern-ness', the instrument's material presence on the soundtrack is really where its 'Eastern-ness' resides. The

Kaidan: radical scoring and ruthless asynchronism

shakuhachi that recurs throughout *The Woman in the Snow* sonically
falls between the cracks of sound, music and noise. Firstly, the
shakuhachi is one of a number of Japanese instruments that intentionally
embrace noise: part of its performance mode is to bring an excess of
breath pressure on the reed to traumatise its otherwise pure tone.
Secondly, the reverberant recording of its performance intensifies the
noise effect by inducing what at times sounds remarkably like ring

modulation distortion. At any one moment, the *shakuhachi* shifts wildly from a conservative lilt to an alien spasm; from an ancient wooden instrument to a post-industrial electronic weapon. In *Kaidan*, this poetically syncs to its highly modernist film reworking traditional folk tales.

The most horrifying of *Kaidan*'s quartet of terror is *Hoichi the Earless*. Blind minstrel Yasaku (Kunie Tanaka) unwittingly sings tales of a grand sea battle so well that his voice summons the battle's ghosts, who in turn summon him to sing for them at their grand court. Not knowing he is performing for the dead, Yasaku regales them with an epic musical romance of their past exploits. When Yasaku's priests discover this, they paint ritual prayers all over his body to render him invisible to the ghosts – except they forget to paint his ears. It's not by accident that a film with such a radical score intensely mocks those who forget they have ears.

Dir: Masaki Kobayashi; **Prod:** Shigeru Wakatsuki; **Scr:** Yoko Mizuki; **DOP:** Yoshio Miyjima; **Editor:** Hisashi Sagara; **Score:** Toru Takemitsu; **Sound:** Hideo Nishizaki; **Main Cast:** Rentaro Mikuni, Michiyo Aratama, Misako Watanabe, Tatsuya Nakadai, Keiko Kishi, Katsuo Nakamura, Tetsuro Tamba.

The Keep
US, 1983 – 96 mins
Michael Mann

Most uses of synthesisers are predicated on the instrument's ability to 'synthesise' an existing instrument. Orchestral string sections have been a designated preset on just about every synthesiser invented, inducing a viral rash of lazy applications of the instrument which mimic, ape and crow brief chordal sequences from the great Romantic unconsciousness to trigger Pavlovian sighs from the audience. Cinema has gulped this down, addicted to the synthesiser's expedient delivery and its kitsch aroma.

Superficially, the all-synthesiser score to *The Keep* performs similarly. But the score's electronic tone deliberately runs counter to its story, set during the spreading Axis occupation of Europe during World War II. Furthermore, the locations and staging of the film are bereft of clear historical signifiers and icons: the granite Carpathanian mountains appear as they would today and 100 years ago; village peasants look localised and timeless; and Glaeken Trismegestus (Lance Henriksen) is posed as an impassive, taciturn figure who moves through darkened caves in search of an evil 'essence' which the Nazis seek to colonise. This pan-generic ahistorical dissolving of details into non-specific settings is enhanced by the score's dissolution of historically weighted textures (the synthesisers' orchestral visage) into a stream of meta-music freed from expected idioms and vernacular.

While many other scores employing synthesisers are intent on merely approximating a vague orchestral effect, *The Keep* noticeably diffuses the orchestral aura as a means of suggesting that the score itself is somehow being transformed. A fine line, but one that is discernible in both the story's centrality of evil as an ungovernable presence, and the constancy and consistency of the music's tenor in symbolising this. The synthesiser's continual melting and morphing of flutes, voices, strings and muted horns into a rich roux characterises it as a non-definable, distanced instrument, devoid of its own identity yet capable of calling up simulated timbres in a breathy, hazy way.

Consequently, *The Keep*'s 'cues' neither rest nor perform as they do in conventionally composed scores. Rather than romantically replicating the dramatic shape of a scene, passages in *The Keep* sculpt icy backdrops and cool facades that simply take place and space within a scene. Within the sometimes massive, sometimes filamental floss of orchestral fibre, one experiences indifference, asynchronism, amorphousness and transcendentalism as cycling and rising four-chord motifs virtually hover still while the film narrative moves through them. An overall passivity and detachment is drawn throughout, serving to accent drama while flattening its envelopes and peaks as simplistic yet dense chordal textures connote an 'orchestra-ness' while emptying the screen soundspace of any true orchestral presence. Thematically, these effects append to the pervasive evil which floats through the film like an unfixed dramatic presence: the score's withholding of dramatic articulation is pertinent.

Dir: Michael Mann; **Prod:** Gene Kirkwood, Howard W. Koch Jr; **Scr:** Michael Mann; **DOP:** Alex Thomson; **Editor:** Dov Hoenig; **Score:** Tangerine Dream; **Sound Editor:** William Trent; **Main Cast:** Scott Glenn, Alberta Watson, Jürgen Prochnow, Robert Prosky, Gabriel Byrne.

Koyaanisqatsi
US, 1982 – 87 mins
Godfrey Reggio

Koyaanisqatsi is well regarded as a synaesthetic overload and
metaphorically linked to superfluous notions of trippy, druggy and
blissed-out states. Despite the hold the film has on those so predisposed,
Koyaanisqatsi's audiovisual bombast is nonetheless complexly founded on
a dialogue between the thunderous density of its orchestra score and the
beautifully degravitised momentum of its stop-motion cinematography.
The film's unending bodies strewn like visceral architecture elicit a precise
emotional response atypical of notions of beings enveloped by music:
less symbols of the transcendental act of listening, they are deaf to the
power of music which trumpets around them. As innocents snared by
the forces of 'life out of balance', these people (not actors) neither react
to it nor sympathise with the music in which they appear to sink. The
score's minimalist quagmire is a deliberately excessive concoction of
boom, gloom and doom. It plays with deafening density, like an
orchestral machine whose every control is set to full energy level and
incapable of being turned off. Far from experiencing the luxury of
transcendence, the films' oppressed denizens of exploited cultures are
coloured with a helplessness courtesy of this omnipresent music which
casts them out of balance with the film score.

Many are understandably overwhelmed by the powerfully emotional
images in *Koyaanisqatsi*, often attributing the meld of music and image
as a sublime fusion. But the film presents a tactic of contra-scoring – one
based on decimating the world it musically illustrates. No slight tinkling
of fey melodies to suggest the frailty of human life here. In its place, we
have dread-inducing collisions between a screaming chorus of heavenly
angels, a massive ground swell of subterranean crypt organs, and the
impression of an impossibly enlarged string section. Patrons leave the
cinema shell-shocked by the music, blasted as much by its incessant
nature as its volume. More than another tasteful tailoring of minimalist

style, here is the orchestra as a post-modern inversion of machinic excess: its majesty and beauty is hyper-referenced in such full-effect that it erodes at its own foundations. *Koyaanisqatsi*'s score pictures a peculiar site of dimensional restructuring, centred on reconfigured zones which superbly imagine that most elusive transcendent state: the point when one shifts from listening to music to being terrorised by its presence.

The excessively rich minimalism which complements the optical pyrotechnics of *Koyaanisqatsi* is not to be dismissed on grounds of its cinesonic overdrive. Sited at an immense crater caused by industrialisation in the name of civilisation, and exploitation under the guise of resourcefulness, the morality of the music's role as commentator is tactfully dispassionate despite its abundance of emotional signifiers. Many have interpreted this as a 'cold' post-modern visage. But it can also be considered as an inversion of the classical chorus of Greek tragedy: instead of the chorus representing angels throwing a life-line to mortals to prevent them from carrying out fateful actions, the score to *Koyaanisqatsi* represents the angels with their backs turned, deaf to the pleas of mortals. The symbolic message bellowed through their operatic monumentalism is frighteningly cursive: it's your world – you made it – now live in it.

Dir: Godfrey Reggio; **Prod:** Godfrey Reggio; **Scr:** Ron Fricke, Michael Hoenig, Godfrey Reggio, Alton Walpole; **DOP:** Ron Fricke; **Editor:** Ron Fricke, Alton Walpole; **Score:** Phillip Glass; **Sound Effects Editor:** David Rivas.

Last Year at Marienbad (*L'Année dernière à Marienbad*)
France, 1959 – 97 mins
Alain Resnais

Last Year at Marienbad is emblematic of *noveau roman* cinema, its literary dissolution of cinema dislocating and preventing one from holding onto rational significance through the film's decimation of conventional audiovisual narration. It has less an actual plot than a meta-plot, colliding time frames, characters behaving as 'semes', and perverse self-awareness bearing little reference to any imaginable social reality.

In *Last Year at Marienbad*, these components are translated into cinematic language through a dialectical relationship between sound and image, wherein the soundtrack creates tensions and ambiguities by playing against the image-track. Mostly, this is conveyed by voiceover narration underscoring, undercutting and undermining the supposed 'truth value' of what we are witness to in the film's images. During the film's hysterical ride through confused emotions which arise from fractured relationships, repressed memories and problematised desires, voiceovers follow infinite colons of baroque architecture (visually symbolising this hysteria) and bouts of theatrical melodrama (foregrounding the stylised means through which the actors enact their scenarios, often gesturing and posturing in stilted tableau fashion).

This merger of palpable poetics with dry dialectics forms a sado-masochistic dance with narration – one that entrances with its complexity. From the outset, voiceover fades up and down as the camera glides and turns into multiplied corridors. Repeated phrases appear to be slight variations in describing non-specific spaces, inflicting an erotic suggestiveness as to who is narrating and why. But just as neither the architecture nor the editing of the framed spatialisations conveys linear or causal logic, so does voiceover refuse to fix itself to any one place. The film's endless tracking shots are symbolic of how voiceover acoustically

Last Year at Marienbad: a sado-masochistic dance with narration

floats down corridors and into spaces, as if in answer to the quandary: if voiceover is a mental projection, how can it be rendered sonic?

Dialogue is similarly collapsed, treated not as information passed between characters, but as points of their disassociation. Typical of how social gatherings function, audiovisual continuity in the film's many party scenes is archly broken. People suddenly freeze en masse in a tableau of interaction; or they are clearly shown to be talking, but the soundtrack mix selectively gives us fragments of what they are saying. Sometimes characters talk at each other rather than to each other; other times characters in isolation passionately talk to someone who isn't there with them. On some occasions, there are transitions between these modes. Psychological tension mounts as we try to either fill in the gaps of silence with meaningful content, or attempt to attach a logical significance to this deliberately fractured audiovisual continuum.

The swelling organ concerto of *Last Year at Marienbad*'s score wraps the voiceover and carries it through architectural and narrative passages of the film. Mix levels between the two heighten tension (when the organ overwhelms the voice) and provide an illusory respite (when the organ dissolves behind the voice). Apparently aleatory in tone and flow, this relationship between organ and voice exemplifies the film's employment of melodrama: a joining of *melo* – music – with *drama* – action. As the music swirls in an onanistic embrace with its compulsion to modulate key, it perfectly scores the mania for and of desire which overwhelms the film's characters.

Dir: Alain Resnais; **Prod:** Pierre Courau, Raymond Froment; **Scr:** Alain Resnais, Alain Robbe-Grillet; **DOP:** Sacha Vierny; **Editor:** Jasmine Chasney, Henri Colpi; **Score:** Francis Seyrig; **Sound:** Guy Villette; **Main Cast:** Delphine Seyrig, Giorgio Albertazzi, Sacha Pitoëff.

Lost Highway
US, 1997 – 135 mins
David Lynch

An intensely quiet moment happens twenty minutes into *Lost Highway*. Fred Madison (Pullman) stands in front of an undefined space, rendered indistinct by the screen's disorienting flatness. As Madison walks forwards into darkness, one becomes acutely sensitised to the sound of his apartment: a humming tone that says nothing is occurring but the ringing rumble of space itself. Location sound recordists refer to it as room tone: texture that has to be recorded separately as filler for dialogue editors, so they may seamlessly segue between passages of recorded speech. Without this sound of nothingness, location dialogue would be revealed in truth as bits wrought from a real 'live' space – too full and present for the audio track's tightly controlled reduction of detail. Dialogue editing, traditionally, must disguise the fact that a real room exists – paradoxically by ensuring that you can't relate its sonic texture of virtual silence to actual silence.

But the strange sonic nothingness in Madison's apartment is thick, fibrous, lichenal. It and other environments in the film are layered with an excess of nothingness, building a dense bed of rumbling tone which lugubriously bleeds into the air-conditioned atmosphere of the cinema itself. Standard practice in mix-down situations is to audition the final mix against a simulated distant traffic rumble to replicate the urban theatre environment so one can check the soundtrack's clarity. *Lost Highway*'s sound design privileges that very substance which the soundtrack figures as noise. Oppressively empty spaces, rooms, chambers and corridors breathe and heave their nothingness through a network of zones vibrating with noisy silence: tensile ringing of fluoro tubes, baritone choruses of central heating, organific tone clusters of electrical circuitry, dissonant harmonics of air vents. The on-screen world is effectively mirrored to inhabit the auditorium – a device well suited to a film whose narrative loops back on itself in an unending nightmare of psychosis.

Elsewhere, *Lost Highway* is bombastic, from the pummelling drives down its darkened highways, to the neo-Gothic guttural groans imbedded in its frighteningly loud music mix. Along with intermittent subsonic booms and explosive cracks, these are the expected traits of the swirling post-modernist noir which typifies the film's openly lurid storytelling. Yet for all the film's noise and volume, the ill ease of its psychodrama is most felt in quieter moments.

The film's 'aural chiaroscuro' continually dissolves the archly dramatic boom into a tactile, sonar tempura which coats the darkened chambers of its locations. Booms are percussive: discrete events which dramatically punctuate a point within the narrative. Drones take the vertical energy of those moments and flatten them into a horizontal spread of de-dramatised continuity. Monotonic drones always create tension because time passes while the 'music' seems to be standing still: the gears are locked and something is stuck. Aptly, *Lost Highway* is about the locked moment of becoming lost – the point at which one crosses over from the known into the unknown; from the deafening roar of that which is happening to the deadly quiet of that which is about to happen.

Dir: David Lynch; **Prod:** Deepak Nayar, Tom Sternberg, Mary Sweeney; **Scr:** David Lynch, Barry Gifford; **DOP:** Peter Deming; **Editor:** Mary Sweeney; **Score:** Angelo Badalamenti; **Sourced Score:** Barry Adamson; **Songs:** David Bowie, Trent Reznor, NIN, Marilyn Manson, Ramstein, Screamin' Jay Hawkins; **Sound Design:** David Lynch; **Main Cast:** Bill Pullman, Patricia Arquette, Balthazar Getty, Robert Blake, Gary Busey, Robert Loggia.

M
Germany, 1931 – 117 mins
Fritz Lang

For a film made so near to the technological advent of sound in the cinema, *M* bears a sophistication in its sound design unmatched by other 'psycho' films of its time as well as many made since. The film is highly designed in its visuals and gesturally ornate in its camera work, and the sound to *M* shares similar weight in its formalist expression and poetic symbolism.

Its binary relationship between sound and silence marks *M* as a pivotal film connecting silent cinema to the then-new sound cinema. Constituted as a bi-morphic narrative, *M* projects sound onto silent form, and cuts silence into sound language. Less a balance and more a twisting of two modes into one thread, it actions sound and silence in direct response to the story's themes. In the chilling tale of paedophile Hans (Lorre), the letter 'M' signifies the sign of the marked man whose time is up in the realm of citizens and criminals alike. Internally scarred by his psychotic disposition, Hans transgresses both realms through his murderous actions, and comes to bear the 'M' on his back: invisible to him as his actions had been to those around him. When eventually tried not by a law court but by a den of criminals with their own codes, Hans claims that the power within that drove him to murder children 'silently follows' him 'through the streets'. This silence accounts for the many ways in which the film uses silence up to its conclusion.

The first instance of a lost child is introduced when Madame Beckmann (Ellen Widmann) waits for her child Elsie to return home for lunch. A series of sonic irritants rupture the silence of the home: a cuckoo clock; a door bell; children running up stairs – but each is a sign of the absence of her Elsie. Across shots of the stairwell and courtyard, her voice calls for Elsie, again and again, until silence occupies the soundtrack, signalling Elsie's death. The police embark on a large-scale manhunt to find Elsie's kidnapper, but their visual descriptions and assumptions lead to nothing but a cacophony of false accusations.

Meanwhile, Hans floats in the midst of the hub-bub, whistling a refrain from *Peer Gynt*. While everyone is looking, they of course should be listening: Hans' loss of control over his own pathological urges is sounded through the way he modulates the melody, expressing urgency, anxiety and arousal in its peak. As deaf to his whistling as are the noisy threatened townsfolk around him, Hans comes to feel an omnipotence associated with serial killers who hide in the light of those seeking them. In total silence, he writes his taunting letters to the police, announcing himself without mouthing his identity. Similarly, his whistling, writing and thinking are all cut to a deadly silence when he is unexpectedly struck by the image of a child framed in a mirror: the terror of his desire invisibly confronts him in the voiceless visage of his next victim. Other dark ironies of silence move in on Hans: the first person to identify him as the killer is a blind man who remembers him whistling; Hans gives himself away to the criminals through his tapping; and with Hans' death, silence no longer enshrouds the city.

Dir: Fritz Lang; **Prod:** Seymour Nebenzal; **Scr:** Paul Falkenberg, Adolf Jansen, Fritz Lang, Karl Vash, Thea von Harbou; **DOP:** Fritz Arno Wagner; **Editor:** Paul Falkenberg; **Sourced Score:** Edvard Grieg; **Sound:** Adolf Jansen; **Main Cast:** Peter Lorre, Gustaf Gründgens, Paul Kemp, Theodor Loos.

Magnolia
US, 1999 – 181 mins
Paul Thomas Anderson

In the weaving and ducking of *Magnolia*'s introductory character-based
movement, so much is told with such an excess of simultaneity, you lose
sense of narrative linkage and progression. During this, Aimee Mann's
cover version of Harry Nilsson's 'One' occupies both screen and
auditorium in a radical way. The soundtrack ducks and weaves all its
elements within and without the architecsonic domain of 'One' in a
flagrant disregard for hierarchical logic in sound design: Mann's 'lead
vocals' mostly ride atop, yet at times even her voice is clouded by the
film's dialogue and the song's own baroque vocal arrangements.

A vocal schizophrenia is orchestrated, following through with a
chorus of expressive utterances breathing in a continually morphing
sonorum which is, literally, breathtaking. All characters are at some point
out of breath, rushing headlong into eruption. *Magnolia* features many
show pieces where vocalisation and legibility precariously come near to
cancelling each other out – consciously so because the flow lines of
character energy in *Magnolia* chart the ways in which characters are
running out of time as their connections with each other contract into a
net of inescapable embraces and releases.

The mix of *Magnolia* is crucial to the film's habitation of one's aural
consciousness. Many characters in the film quote, 'You may be done
with the past, but the past is not done with you', and the film
accordingly lives simultaneously in its past and in its present. On many
occasions, multiple musics occur simultaneously, creating circles of
dissonance which radiate through the auditorium. *Magnolia*'s characters
are not 'vessels': they are amplifiers, speakers and transmitters of
psychodrama; the theatre becomes a noisy ward within which you are
interred.

(Opposite page) Magnolia: orchestrating a vocal schizophrenia

Cancer, of course, is the draining life force of *Magnolia*. Epicentral is the bizarre audiovisual zoom into the decaying throat of Earl Partridge (Robards) as he hoarsely whispers through the frenetic cellular activity which signals his body's surrender. Just as you virtually smell death on his breath, you can feel its presence on your own eardrums. All key emotional points performance-wise are similarly presented through debilitating inversions of vocal power: Mrs Partridge (Moore) provides numerous black holes of gasping and gnashing as she deals with Earl's demise; Frank Mackie (Cruise) breathlessly vomits years of hatred over Earl on his death bed; Claudia (Walters) vents a volcanic ocean of steaming rage when her father Jimmy Gator (Hall) intrudes upon her frail sanctity. Just as Partridge is himself a cancerous cell in the glandular familial spread of all the film's characters, so too does each and every person expel and repeat his infected breath one remove from their own emotional death.

Magnolia's sound design follows this deigned cancerous spread: voices and music leak through thin walls; TVs crackle indifferently, indignantly and incessantly, oxidising the most private domains; car sound systems carry their passengers within their subsonic wombs; music cues well up and spill over into scenes for which they were destined as well as those poised innocently adjacent; and radio playlists infect public spaces like a cold in an air-conditioned office. Sound in *Magnolia* is thus mostly about that which you wish to suppress, engaging you in a wearing psychoacoustic fight: you strain to hear, you wish for silence, you attempt to focus, you achieve your own noise threshold.

Dir: Paul Thomas Anderson; **Prod:** Paul Thomas Anderson, Joanne Sellar; **Scr:** Paul Thomas Anderson; **DOP:** Robert Elswit; **Editor:** Dylan Tichenor; **Score:** John Brion; **Song Score:** Aimee Mann; **Sourced Songs:** Supertramp; **Sourced Score:** Giacomo Puccini; **Sound Design:** Richard King; **Main Cast:** John C. Reilly, Tom Cruise, Julianne Moore, Philip Baker Hall, Jeremy Blackman, Philip Seymour Hoffman, William H. Macy, Melora Walters, Jason Robards, Melinda Dillon.

The Man Who Lies (*L'Homme qui ment*)
France, 1968 – 95 mins
Alain Robbe-Grillet

Surely the most honest thing is to declare one's lie as one is stating it. Yet at such a moment of utterance, the split between truth and falsehood evaporates into a mist of assumptions, interpretations and possibilities. *The Man Who Lies* presents such a scenario. Across title credits, a man appears to be chased through a forest. Eventually his flight is intercut with shots of German soldiers and their panting Alsatians. Gunfire and barking dogs are heard near and far. The man reaches a clearing; a loud gunshot ruptures the soundtrack; he falls down. The camera moves up to him and looks down on his face; his eyes open – then he gets up and nonchalantly walks away.

Within this 'film that lies' a story precariously unfolds. *The Man Who Lies* is set some time after World War II somewhere in France. Boris (Trintignant) wanders aimlessly through a small village previously occupied by the German army. He calls upon people there, soliciting their memory of his involvement in the resistance movement. Continually he says, 'Let me tell you my story', but modifies it each time, sometimes giving himself a different name. He prods people: 'You were there – surely you remember me'. Before long, every time Boris opens his mouth, one is prepared to hear a convolution of the events, and a confounding of purpose in him telling them.

Such is the nature of dialogue in *The Man Who Lies*. Less about exchange and interaction, speech is a device to dissolve truth. The act of speaking forms a fabricated amalgam of assertion, bias and partiality. The film coherently employs sound as a means to query its image, sometimes playfully and sometimes confrontationally, but always wrenching one from the other's cling. The overall purpose is to create a world where multiple subjectivities collide; where the central narration of Boris is unrooted and set loose.

Boris is mostly met with silence by others. They are initially posed as strangely detached mutes, on whose deaf ears Boris' versions fall. This grows to such an extent one can perceive Boris as sealed in his own hermetic world. But rather than this being a symbolic gesture towards alienation of the traumatised post-war psyche, the cinematic construction of *The Man Who Lies* presents Boris' world as one that intersects with and problematises the representational world on the screen. That is, the image – and consequently, the sound – of Boris is entirely divorced from the depicted realm which he appears to be inhabiting with others. His presence is a disturbance; his countenance, stature, eye-line, motion and gesture all disconnect from others; the sound of his footsteps, the wind he hears, the music he encounters – all are interferences to the scenes he illusorily haunts. Like a post-war ghost wandering through a shell-shocked domain, he is potentially a figure others wish to forget: a name they wish they had never heard, no matter how many times he changes it. Ultimately, the film shifts the misleading slant of its story: the French villagers wish that Boris is indeed the man who lies. But his rupturing of their world – as conveyed through the meticulous subversion of sound–image veracity and synchronism – sites him in a film that does not lie.

Dir: Alain Robbe-Grillet; **Prod:** Jan Tomaskovic; **Scr:** Alain Robbe-Grillet; **DOP:** Igor Luther; **Editor:** Bob Wade; **Sound:** Michel Fano; **Main Cast:** Sylvie Bréal, Zuzana Kocúriková, Jozef Kroner, Ivan Mistrík, Dominique Prado, Jean-Louis Trintignant.

Metropolis
Germany/US, 1926 and 1983 – 120 mins
Fritz Lang

Flickering like an old silent movie, yet bathed in a saturated hue of gold, this 1983 reconstruction of *Metropolis* commences with a series of intertitles explaining the film's historical and mythical importance. Throughout, a pulsing electronic robo-disco beat grows in volume. With the official credit 'constructed and adapted by Giorgio Moroder', this *Metropolis* is bound to outrage the conservative cinephile. Mirroring the film's creation of the Maria robot, 'versioning' was the norm in silent cinema musical accompaniment, and *Metropolis* – despite being enshrined for its originality – is an infamous instance of exactly how replication and duplication governed cinema distribution in the 20s. Linking expressionist technopia with MTV golden era ersatz, *Metropolis* simultaneously acknowledges the greatness of past art and reinvents it as a modern faddish event.

Ethical and taste considerations aside, this new version affords a rare opportunity to audit the effects of removing one score and totally replacing it with a comparatively alien and dislocating one. Of particular note is how the aural/musical rhythms of the score are often at odds with a scene's visual frame dynamics and its edited shape. The 'MTV effect' comes to the fore in this respect: songs either scream their synchronism (Bonnie Tyler screeching 'She's the Same – But She's Different' when the evil Maria preaches to the workers in the catacombs) or indifferently waft across whole scenes (the depiction of the Garden of Delights). Simulating the watching of TV with the sound turned down while listening to a CD, this 'hit-or-miss' matching momentarily denotes mistiming, yet holistically tends to an elasticised sense of timing. It is this type of stretchable timing that characterised silent cinema before the mechanical soundtrack metronomically locked picture to sound. While appearing to be cavalier and throwaway with its 'cues', *Metropolis* is possibly a more apt version than the many historically 'authentic' versions which have claimed veracity in their formal construction.

A key to *Metropolis*' delight lies in the way the soundtrack's now-dated modernism has 'curdled' the image-track's once-glorious modernism. Seeing the crumpled fabric of the workers' uniforms and their white faces evokes a theatre space typical of much silent cinema, where the surface of people and materials has a pre-cinematised aura. The camera works to anthropologically document the staged performances rather than transform them into a photogenic apparition. Hearing the analogue synthesiser score achingly shoots one into the early 80s and that era's sonic future signalled by banks of sequenced synthesisers. More than a post-modern proposition, this meeting of sound and image creates a warp point which separates the futurist projection from the 20s with a backwards (i.e. pre-digital) sonic trajectory from the 80s. Both miss their mark, yet in doing so draw a zone that contains their opposed trajectories. Then again, this may be a mere matter of confounded expectations: many films set in ancient times feature 'forward' music from the 18th century, yet seem to absolve themselves from audiovisual disjuncture.

Dir: Fritz Lang; **Prod:** Erich Pommer; **Scr:** Fritz Lang, Thea von Harbou; **DOP:** Karl Freund, Günther Rittau; **Editor:** uncredited; **Adaptation and Reconstruction:** Girogio Moroder; **Re-scored Songs:** Giorgio Moroder; **Main Cast:** Alfred Abel, Gustav Fröhlich, Brigitte Helm, Rudolf Klein-Rogge.

Oedipus Rex (*Edipo re*)
Italy, 1967 – 110 mins
Pier Paolo Pasolini

A contemporary trend in music selection for film is to thread the disparate musical semes of transient and dislocated musical cultures into a global homogeneous narrative. Under the rubric of 'world music', gypsy tarantellas, enka ballads and sufi wailing have accompanied just about any humanist scenario under the guise of a musicological 'family of man' principle.

Pre-dating and opposed to such manoeuvres, *Oedipus Rex* accords different musical styles their individual and separate status by connecting them to a chain of heterogeneous events. Ironically, this occurs as these musical cues are set to a filmed version of a grand mythological narrative: the Oedipus tale. Heterogeneity is always apparent due to the anti-narrative techniques employed in the film: discontinuous editing; partially defined settings and alienating landscapes; brutish, improvised documentary-style camera work; a pot-pourri of performance modes from trained actors and on-site locals; and post-synced dialogue tracks devoid of original location atmosphere. An overall logic of linear and lateral collage governs not only how music attaches itself to image, but also how it separates itself from preceding and proceeding musical segments. It is this process of differentiation that defines *Oedipus Rex*'s musicological programme.

In place of music being employed to speciously voice that which is 'in us all', *Oedipus Rex*'s music is always felt to come from 'somewhere else'. Early in the film, the Oedipal baby wanders to the edge of a balcony, attracted to a foxtrot record playing in a room across the plaza where his mother dances with a soldier. This sets up a recurring figure of Oedipus wandering into terrains and situations where music is already playing. Despite the music never once matching the authenticity of either the film's scenography or the story's mythology, its internment on the soundtrack gives the music its place regardless.

Oedipus Rex: music felt to have come from somewhere else

This is a major inverse of the orthodox practice of 'correct' musicological supervision, where place (setting, location, etc.) determines the music.

These musicological 'attachments' resonate with poetic curvature (the mother breast-feeding the Italian baby to the strains of a sombre string quartet; victims of pestilence being burnt as we hear a deep male chorus; children's rhyme-singing as Polybus and the Queen look upon the newly found Oedipus; etc.) and psychological tension (Japanese solo flute as Teiresias the prophet confronts Oedipus with truth; Indonesian vocal chants as Oedipus encounters a frightening naked woman inside mudbrick corridors; etc.). Like Oedipus' looped fatalistic arcs which return him to scenes of his crimes and misdemeanours, the musical attachments are appended to multiple scenes, creating unsettling echoes without ever fixing musical sense to any one musical placement.

Essentially, *Oedipus Rex* is a disturbing text, founded not simply on its core mythic taboo, but more on the inescapability of one's bearing witness to one's own deeds. When Oedipus stabs his eyes out after he sees his wife/mother has hung herself, he voices the totalising audiovisual terror which has dictated the film's soundtrack: 'I should have cut off my ears too, to better lock away my wretched body and to no longer see or hear anything'.

Dir: Pier Paolo Pasolini; **Prod:** Alfredo Bini; **Scr:** Luigi Scaccianoce; **DOP:** Giuseppe Ruzzolini; **Editor:** Nino Baragli; **Sound:** Carlo Tarc; **Main Cast:** Silvana Mangano, Franco Citti, Alida Valli, Carmelo Bene, Julian Beck.

Once Upon a Time in the West (C'era una volta il west)
Italy, 1969 – 165 mins
Sergio Leone

The long opening to *Once Upon a Time in the West* is notable for its absence of dialogue, wherein it is difficult not to perceive the complex filigree of sonic and silent filaments tensely strung across the widescreen. But this is not special in the realm of Italian Westerns, which – counter to the delicious loquaciousness of Italian cinema – feature stoic gunmen of few words. This opening scene has a specific logic to its extenuation of silence and suppression of vocalisation.

As three dusters wait for a train, they bide their time in unfolding order. Firstly, these are hired guns, waiting for their victim to arrive by train. Psychotically disposed, each spends his time not fretfully but calmly, mentally preparing for their murderous task. The surrounding landscape provides a master clock – the creaking windmill – for their individual patterns. Snaky (Jack Elam) slouches half-asleep; Stony (Woody Strode) stands in total silence; and Knuckles (Al Mulock) fidgets, cracking his knuckles. Secondly, their 'psycho-rhythms' are counterpointed by sonic occurrences: the telegraph Snaky silences by destroying it; the fly he captures in his gun barrel; and the water dripping onto Stony's forehead which he transforms into a dull, calming pulse by putting on his hat.

The scream of the train whistle pierces their hermetic sound fields. When the train comes to rest, it chugs ominously with a heaving rhythm that now replaces all others. As the dusters are about to leave, a wailing harmonica – complete with distended reverb – cuts through the train's steamy surges. The dusters' response matches our double-take: is this 'noise' score or diegetic sound? Harmonica (Bronson) emerges through the steam like an avenging angel, harmonica in mouth, breathing it to play his signature seething which symbolises the revenge he seeks.

Many instances of musical grandeur and thematic orchestration dance across the opulent soundtrack to *Once Upon a Time in the West*:

the warm waltz and its cascading arrangement which choreograph Jill's (Cardinale) reveries; the 'clip-clop' banjo pluck which hiccups along to loveably amoral Cheyenne's (Robards) numerous double-crosses; the dark fuzz guitar riff which vibrates down the inhuman backbone of Frank (Fonda).

Yet they all whirl round the harmonica's morbid leitmotiv. It lives as aberrant aural sign and composed musical device. Its three-note refrain atomises both the high-pitched train whistle (symbolising the owner of the train company, Morton (Ferzetti), who hired Frank to kill Harmonica's brother) and the score's central cycling motif played by mournful horns. It also expresses – literally – the sound Harmonica heard while he was forced to play it as his brother was hung. Harmonica thus becomes his harmonica, wearing it around his neck like a dead albatross. In the matching of his long, extreme close-up to distant drawn-out violins mimicking the motif, Harmonica stiffly inhales the instrument's dissonant odour each time he exacts revenge on all complicit in his brother's death. Not wholly a doomed figure, Harmonica finds closure when he thrusts his harmonica into the mouth of Frank in a sublime act of transference. Only when Harmonica can hear that same sound wheezing through the dying lips of Frank can he relinquish the hold of its noise.

Dir: Sergio Leone; **Prod:** Fulvio Morsella; **Scr:** Dario Argento, Bernardo Bertolucci, Sergio Donati, Mickey Knox, Sergio Leone; **DOP:** Tonino Delli Colli; **Editor:** Nino Baragli; **Score:** Ennio Morricone; **Sound Effects:** Luciano Anzellotti, Roberto Arcangeli, Italo Cameracanna; **Main Cast:** Charles Bronson, Henry Fonda, Claudia Cardinale, Jason Robards, Gabriele Ferzetti.

Patty Hearst
US, 1988 – 108 mins
Paul Schrader

Cinematic portrayals of mind control lend themselves to extreme manipulations of sound–image relationships. *Patty Hearst* goes quite far in this regard. Detailing the disorientation, decline and deprogramming of Patty Hearst (Richardson) from heiress to militant, the film is shattered into myriadfold psychological shards, each constituting a torn fragment of her psyche. Her sense of self, location and place – in both personal/physical and social/political terms – is reconfigured, and expressed through a mind-cleansing reprogramming of that which is presumed to be a 'balanced' mix of sound and image.

The ripping of sound from image is overt in the extended sequences where Patty is locked in a cupboard by her kidnappers, the Symbionese Liberation Army. In the cupboard's suffocating blackness, she is utterly alone in what becomes an ever-expanding void as she gradually transforms her sense of being. The darkness – noted as a refusal of cinematic image – removes her sight and thus her primarily encoded relation to the world: nothing is visible, therefore nothing exists out there. Wrenched from its domain, her voice is the only marker of self within the cupboard's nothingness. More than intensely gazing into a mirror – a typical cinematic device to show a character's awareness of self at a remove – she responds to her own voice as if perceiving something deep within herself. The texture and presence of her voice is thus foregrounded as its own psychological universe throughout these scenes. Sound, also, becomes the thread for her sanity: sight – gained only by violent bursts of white light when the door is periodically opened by silhouetted guards – terrorises, invades and assaults her de-socialised space. Her sensorial world is turned upside down: sound precedes, writes, frames and actions image.

To reflect the swirling madness that rages around Patty's desensitisation, *Patty Hearst*'s score is a musicalised exploration and denotation of her voice. Semi-atonal phrases appear incongruous until one realises they are based on studying the chromatic pitch rises and falls in Patty's spoken words. Phrases like 'mom, dad' and 'I'm not being held by force' are reconstituted as unique melodies – replayed within the film just as Patty's words are played to her parents and the FBI. Both misrecognise her voice: mom and dad incapable of 'seeing' her within her words and actions; the FBI incapable of 'seeing' what conspiratorial and manipulative forces are controlling her. While Patty's voice is interpreted as being that of a ventriloquist's dummy – not 'our' Patty, the Patty of her 'others' – her fractured voice is the result of an imposed journey of self-discovery (whether she wants it or not). The music's diverse complexity, angular harmonies and contra-rhythmic manifestation vividly represent this 'divorced self' which Patty becomes – disowned by everyone including herself.

Dir: Paul Schrader; Prod: Marvin Worth; Scr: Nicholas Kazan; DOP: Bojan Bazelli; Editor: Michael R. Miller; Score: Scott Johnson; Supervising Sound Editor: Michael Kirchberger; Main Cast: Natasha Richardson, William Forsythe, Ving Rhames, Frances Fisher, Jodi Long, Olivia Barash.

The Pawnbroker
US, 1965 – 116 mins
Sidney Lumet

Blackness – as much a virulent, adaptable amoeba as a clear, potent essence – can be felt as muted subsonic waves on the soundtracks of Hollywood's classical cinema. From the smeared jazz of gangster movies to the mottled R&B of Broadway musicals, African-American music squirms like dancing insects under Hollywood's Euro-Caucasian blanket of fiction. Rather then be dismissed as inauthentic tracings of 'true' black music, the irksome pseudo-jitterbuggery which peps Hollywood film scores through the 30s and 40s should be regarded as Hollywood's inability to suppress the sono-musical swell that is black music: offensive to the cultured taste-drums of the time yet too impressive to be aurally absented.

Blackness first oozes from its suppressed depths through the cracks deliberately engineered in social-conscious cinema of the late 50s and early 60s. Reflecting a developing black consciousness that equally affected black and white America, the score for *The Pawnbroker* is among the first dark drops which would eventually allow film scores to sound overtly jazzy and funky. It is notable for its detailed combination of an urban black sensibility with a studied and perfected European-style mode of orchestration. Moments in *The Pawnbroker* deftly and cunningly slide between the two. More than simply an example of unadulterated jazz allowed into the cinematic domain, this score squirms like an unwelcome alien, an ill-fitting being, and declares its displacement clearly. Like a black on the Hollywood soundtrack; like a Jew in Spanish Harlem – Holocaust survivor Sol Nazerman (Steiger) is interred in his pawnbroker cage and desperately eking out an existence in the concentrated encampment of a pressured inner-urban domain. The main title's use of vibes, celeste, harpsichord and harp tantalisingly cast semi-jazz clusters against a monophonic semi-blues line played by thickened strings. It's like hearing Ellington and George Gershwin simultaneously. It's black and it's jazz and all the space between.

The Pawnbroker: a score squirming like an alien

In another sense, it is also funky. Not as in the percolating rhythms which mix erotic downbeats with lazy syncopation into pulsation that we normally associate with funk music, but 'funky' as in a heady brew of extreme contrasts and polyglot textures which celebrate Otherness. Throughout *The Pawnbroker*, that 'melting pot' of which American culture is so proud sweats and breathes. Latin percussion, fusion-style alto-sax solos, be-bop double bass, freestyle drum-kit bursts, atonal organ lines – all played with authentic prowess – capture the mulatto melodiousness of the real and mythical New York street. No aural homogenisation is apparent; multiple instrumental voices are allowed their distinctive presence in the arrangement and the mix.

The Pawnbroker typifies the then-emerging 'sound of the city' as a brash, harsh, violent environment where racial and/or criminal tension is tauter than any violin a soundtrack could record. Strains, glimmers and blasts of soul, R&B, blues, jazz and funk are blended into a beautiful African-American sonorum which wrenches the film score from its Wagnerian cave and slams it down in the midst of cross-town traffic.

Dir: Sidney Lumet; **Prod:** Ely A. Landau, Philip Langner, Roger Lewis, Herbert R. Steinmann; **Scr:** Morton S. Fine, David Friedkin; **DOP:** Boris Kaufman; **Editor:** Ralph Rosenblum; **Score:** Quincy Jones; **Sound Editor:** Jack Fitzstephens, Alan Reim; **Main Cast:** Rod Steiger, Geraldine Fitzgerald, Brock Peters, Jaime Sanchez.

The Pittsburgh Trilogy
US, 1972 – 102 mins
Stan Brakhage

If images can be deafening, *The Pittsburgh Trilogy* is the loudest silent movie ever made. Comprised of three short films (*Eyes*, *Deus Ex* and *The Act of Seeing with One's Own Eyes*), a composite documentary is formed from three observational studies of, respectively, a police patrolman, a hospital doctor, and a coroner in a morgue.

Yet that description is disingenuous. The term 'documentary' curdles and peels away in face of the glowing, throbbing, flexing universe of encoded ephemera dancing on the film's visual surface. A million and one schisms, fluctuations and inconsistencies dynamise that surface – at once suggesting great depth of field in its visually abstracted clouds and optically processed sparkles, while affirming that its universe is as flat as the skin of one's own eye. Like an ocular algae whose slimy dermis works as a prism to refract an uncharted dimension of activity, *The Pittsburgh Trilogy* is not an act of watching: it literally takes over one's eyes. Due to its abject visuality, it cannot afford to entertain a soundtrack. In place, it offers the complete absence of one, and in its radical audiovisual imbalance ontologically queries the role of the soundtrack 'in' or 'upon' the screen.

In line with *The Pittsburgh Trilogy*'s operation as 'an act of seeing', the narrative development through the three films assembles an imagined body as its 'star'. It is a wholly 'screen body' that is first thrown past the transgressive borders patrolled by the law, then interred for repair and servicing within the institution of medicine, then finally set to rest as an assemblage of matter devoid of all life force. This overwhelmingly cinematic body is the corpus of flashes of flesh, bits of bone and moments of muscle which come into contact with a policeman, a doctor, a coroner. The body's trajectory makes a refreshing mockery of 'the hero's journey' by presenting the body as an indistinct, unnamed, anonymous lump. The silence of the film is crucial to this reading of the body's reinstatement as a dumb, mute, inarticulate mass.

Come the third section of the film and its uncompromised image of a corpse's mouth being used to hold its own peeled-back face while its skull is being sawed open for the removal of its brain, the notion of what this film has to say through its characters is perfectly expressed by the sonic reality of our mortality. While the sight of our demise, the stench of our decrepitude and the cold, viscous touch of our putrescence can communicate to the senses of those living, we will not be making a single sound. And that's exactly what you hear in *The Pittsburgh Trilogy*.

Dir: Stan Brakhage; Prod: Stan Brakhage; Scr: Stan Brakhage; DOP: Stan Brakhage; Editor: Stan Brakhage.

Planet of the Apes
US, 1968 – 112 mins
Franklin J. Schaffner

When a film is set in the future, Hollywood tells us that music from another world sounds like twentieth-century avant-garde music. When a film is set in the present, Hollywood tells us that music from the 18th and 19th centuries best describes the present. Apparently, a musicological time warp has defined the dimensional laws of film music throughout the 20th century.

When an astronaut crew passes through a time warp in *Planet of the Apes* and returns to earth in the future, a magically perverse phenomenon occurs: they visit a time where the music is vaguely in sync with the era of the film's production. *Planet of the Apes'* score references the work of Edgar Varèse – in particular, his 1923 work *Hyperprism* for wind instruments and percussion, and his 1954 work *Déserts* for orchestra and magnetic tape. These pieces bracket Varèse's exploration of the sonority of percussion instruments in an era when their identity and purpose were perceived to be suitable mainly for non-melodic dramatic heightening and dynamic pinpointing. Varèse distinctively treated all orchestral instruments as percussive components. *Planet of the Apes'* blend of this tack into its score prompts consideration of how contemporary composition relates to the essentially Romantic apparatus of cinema.

As George Taylor (Heston) and his crew roam the desolate neo-earthscape after crashing into a lake, extensive cinematography documents a terrain which we presume is another planet (as per their stated mission). The score rustles with index-finger piano lines – blunt, stunted, repetitive; shudders of drums and bongos – tense and barely contained convulsions; distant conga finger presses – simulating vowelled sighs. This is the terrain of Apes: spurts of communally excited chattering. The score symbolises this domain which Man has heroically but dumbly transgressed. The irony, of course, is that the Apes are the intelligent force of the future, while Man has retarded into an animalistic existence. The score, then, is Man as ape; its performance and retrogressive composure suggest that musically illiterate brutes have ventured into the orchestral pit and are wreaking havoc with the instruments (an assumption still held of avant-garde music and free jazz alike).

While Varèse's work uses the orchestra to absent Man in the face of Nature's grandeur to celebrate its scope and majesty through expanding one's experience of sound over musical language, *Planet of the Apes* posits such an affair as traumatising. The score's tension does not simply arise from its coded stealth and suspense, but from its fear of Man's loss of articulate control over musical expression. Notably, *Planet of the Apes'* social themes are centred around language and speech: future Man cannot speak while Apes communicate with what was once 'our' language. The use of horns highlights this reversal. Varèse's idiosyncratic approach was to create tetrachords from separate horns playing single notes, each instrument waiting its turn to sustain its note and contribute to the chord's build-up. This effect in *Planet of the Apes* simulates the mono-dimensional groan, bark or grunt which attempts language but cannot string together a series of phonemes to convey meaning. Reduced to choruses of fixed atonal howls, Man and music declare that which Romantic cinema most fears: I have nothing to say.

Dir: Franklin J. Schaffner; **Prod:** Arthur P. Jacobs; **Scr:** Michael Wilson, Rod Serling; **DOP:** Leon Shamroy; **Editor:** Hugh S. Fowler; **Score:** Jerry Goldsmith; **Sound:** David Dockendorf, Herman Lewis; **Main Cast:** Charlton Heston, Roddy McDowall, Kim Hunter, Maurice Evans.

Playtime
France, 1967 – 155 mins
Jacques Tati

Taking aim at affluent post-war Parisians' attraction to new-fangled gadgetry, *Playtime* depicts with humour their life as a strange puppet-like existence. Despite the film's parodic tone, notions of architecture, interior design, urban planning, transport, industrial design, consumerism and the growing leisure industries are studiously reflected. Added to the film's visual distinction is a sound design which incisively critiques how little the aural and the acoustic are considered by designers whose thoughts are formed by image alone.

Playtime heavily manipulates the soundtrack to posit the man–machine interface as the audiovisual core of its cinematic statement, documenting: (a) space; (b) how a body inhabits that space; and (c) what sound that body makes when in that space. Perennial naive wanderer Monsieur Hulot (Tati) embodies this, performing largely in response to sound, rather than – in traditional vaudeville mode – making sound to signify a gag.

Seemingly hyperbolic in its visual design and studio fabrication, *Playtime* 'sounds' all that is absent from realist cinema. The film's ultra-fabrication leads it to consider sound from the ground up, and through such consciousness to realise how much needs to be incorporated to allow the soundtrack to co-habit the visual plane. Whenever Hulot or any character enters a space, we hear them walk, wheel or clatter on distinctively resonating surfaces; if they touch any object – an electric buzzer, a glass door, a plastic folder, a vinyl chair – we perceive the 'sonic character' of that object as well as characters' reactions to it. The opening airport sequence masterfully orchestrates a complete audiovisual vocabulary of modern design with very few legible words uttered. Throughout *Playtime* everyone makes noise, but Hulot alone hears inappropriateness and absurdity in every sonic event. In further evidence of its departure from noisy vaudevillian sight gags, *Playtime* often posits characters grappling with disjunctures between sight and sound, from people interred behind sound-proofed glass to the hilarious invention of the silent door (promoted by the sign 'Slam your door in golden silence').

Inside the Invention Pavilion – a simulacrum of *Playtime*'s commentary – images and sounds become each other. Patrons are confused as to what is real, what is not; what is a model, what is an object; who is a customer, who is an attendant. Blurring the pavilion with its embrace by the outside world, *Playtime* lambastes the specious order imposed on people not only through contraptions and time-saving devices, but also by pneumonic signage, audio communications systems, and piped muzak. The score ironically quotes muzak tropes and blends them with whimsical provençale traits, signifying Hulot's floating innocence as he randomly criss-crosses the hyper-designed pathways of modern Parisian commerce.

Counterpointing this composed ambience is the jazz group at the newly opened nightclub. Their comparatively human and expressive performance becomes score for both the club's collapse and the liberation of its denizens through a set of atmospheric/ambient/sono-musical movements. While the opening to *Playtime* features a drum and organ improv set against empty sky (anthropologically equating jazz with freedom), it closes with carnivalesque muzak mimicking the dinky movements of tourists and traffic, whirling like mass marionettes on a rotating fairground display: a wind-up mechanical Paris offered as respite to its electronic din.

Dir: Jacques Tati; Prod: René Silveera; Scr: Art Buchwald, Jacques Lagrange, Jacques Tati; DOP: Jean Badal, Andréas Winding; Editor: Gérard Pollicand; Score: Francis Lemarque; Sound: Jacques Maumont; Main Cast: Jacques Tati, Barbara Dennek.

(Opposite page) Playtime: sounding all that is absent from realist cinema

Pride of the Marines
US, 1945 – 119 mins
Delmer Daves

Pride of the Marines is centred on Al Schmid's (Garfield) slide from gung-ho cockiness into self-pitying remorse, creating a startling film noir interpolation of a patriotic yet steeling wartime examination of a veteran's condition. The film is exceptional in its focus on the cavernous interiority opened up in Al's psyche when he returns home to his sweetheart Ruth (Parker) after being blinded during battle at Guadalcanal. Rather than dwell on metaphors of sight or excessively verbalise Al's trauma, the film's soundtrack underwrites the heightened aural state which grips Al as he remembers, feels and desires a rounded relationship with the world now sealed off from his vision.

The disjuncture between sight and sound is concentrated at the nexus of Al and Ruth's relationship: we see her – the unseeable object of Al's desire – while he only hears her – triggered by the sound of her presence. A unique voyeuristic conflation is engaged in the perceptual polygon of their emotional connection. Yet sound imparts an ominous portent quite early in the film: from the camera's unsettling focus on the radio as it replays information about the attack on Pearl Harbor, to the deep chimes which undercut the celebrations of the New Year's Eve party.

During the hellish battle at Guadalcanal, the terror of sound over sight comes to the fore. As Al and his buddies are trapped in their foxhole, screams of other soldiers near and far create a sonic net which intensifies their entrapment. Bomb blasts send psychological shock waves through their frayed constitutions, and kinetic juxtapositions between dread-inducing blackness and blinding light destabilise their grip on the situation. Perhaps most unsettling is Al's doomed urging to his buddy, 'Shoot 'em in the eyes'. Soon after, Al is struck by a deadly detonation. His transformative moment is one of audiovisual obliteration: screen and soundtrack are blasted to the extremes of their encoding, symbolising the synaesthetic scarring which will determine his being from this point on. The disorienting *musique concrète* collage which scores Al's later feverish dream in hospital functions like an internal soundtrack to *Pride of the Marines*, mixing its aural components in illustration of the imbalanced world Al now inhabits.

Schmid's road to recovery entails a tug-of-war with himself, intriguingly conveyed by shifts between dialogue and voiceover, and between speech and silence. When Al recovers in hospital before returning home, he dictates a letter for Ruth to his nurse. She prompts him to add 'I love you' which allows him to reach a new level of his projected relationship with Ruth; this moment triggers his voiceover which frames the event within his perspective. Ruth's long-awaited sight of the returned Al leads her and Al to speak around his blindness, while we can see that she is blind to his disability through her love, and that he is blind to the depths of that same love due to his resentment of his disability. The waves of melodrama and pathos which gush through their dialogue desperately attempt to address their fateful kiss on the eve of Al going to war – when they stood in a locked embrace, eyes wide shut, mouths sealing each other, dancing still to a totally silent soundtrack.

Dir: Delmer Daves; **Prod:** Jerry Wald; **Scr:** Marvin Borowsky, Albert Maltz; **DOP:** J. Peverell Marley; **Editor:** Owen Marks; **Score:** Franz Waxman; **Sound:** Stanley Jones; **Main Cast:** John Garfield, Eleanor Parker, Dane Clark, John Ridgely.

Psycho
US 1960 – 104 mins
Alfred Hitchcock

The score to *Psycho* is not to be assumed as accompaniment. The film integrates it and transforms it into a cinesonic substance which fires the film's psychotic expulsions. A richly fetid soundscape operating under the guise of musicality, the atonal edges of this strings-only score decimate any allusions to bellowing nineteenth-century symphonia. This is music strung out on violence, cutting like a wielded blade, and screaming in bouts of rage.

The variable harmonic manifestations of *Psycho*'s score are consistently perverse. It entrances Marion (Leigh) like the swirling sonic smoke of a drug as she wonders what to do with the money she should be banking. It surges forth in manic modulation as her car drives uncontrollably through a maze of forked roads – even transforming her windscreen wipers into hysterical batons forced to slash the rain in time to the score. It beckons her like a timid child's singing, drawing her into the mausoleum which houses 'Mrs Bates'. And finally, it gulps its own palpitations in morbid mimicry of her draining blood swirling down the plughole.

And yet the score continues to control the film past Marion's demise – because the score is the psychic template for how Norman's (Perkins) innate Otherness draws a musical map across a range of uncontrolled and uncontrollable instances. Hence the death of Marion halfway through the film. The themes presumed to be associated with her attach themselves to other innocents – detective Arbogast (Balsam) and Lila (Miles) – as Norman's impulse to kill becomes serial in both psychological and musical terms. The atonal score closely matches his disposition. Insignificant in social stature but absolute in asocial effect, the score's atonality portrays Norman as a self-possessed particle of modern inhumanness.

When Marion is engaged in lengthy conversation with Norman in his private sanctuary, the score gives cue to the schizophrenic nature of

Norman. In one of the most beautiful movements of the score, two lines dissolve into each other: a three-note motif symbolising the mother's hold on Norman, and steaming entrails of serialised melodies which hiss in unpredictable furls, symbolising Norman's mental contortions. The former starts as exceedingly high violins and steps down octaves until it is rendered by dark double cellos; the latter inverts this dynamic, starting as rising cellos and morphing into inaudible kettle-whistling. Every concatenated note matches every word and facial nuance of Norman as he speaks of his departed mother. The movement starts with dread, but ends with calm: maybe Norman is OK after all. But this calm begets the savage takeover of his Other (mother) whose fury wells up in a screeching crescendo of unabashed noise: the orchestra itself is being slashed in a destructive mode befitting the film's modernist reflexive form.

Violins in their romanticised symphonic attire have become emblematic of cinema's epic sweep and heroic grandeur, assailing audiences with grossly amplified beauty requiring hyper categories of kitsch. *Psycho* makes no bones about its attack on the audience: its compositional focus on stringed instruments presents them as objects of necrophilia – carved from a living tree, hollowed out to falsely resonate its human tuning, strung with the guts of an eviscerated cat, and teased erotically by the hair of a dead horse. If the arts are driven to whisper beauty in death, *Psycho* declaims it loudly.

Dir: Alfred Hitchcock; **Prod:** Alfred Hitchcock; **Scr:** Joseph Stefano; **DOP:** John L. Russell; **Editor:** George Tomasini; **Score:** Bernard Herrmann; **Sound:** William Russell, Waldon O. Watson; **Main Cast:** Anthony Perkins, Vera Miles, John Gavin, Martin Balsam, Janet Leigh.

Punch-Drunk Love
US, 2002 – 95 mins
Paul Thomas Anderson

Punch-Drunk Love may appear to reference romantic comedy from a pre-cynical era of cinema, but that is where its cinematic veneer ends. Underneath its mere historical sheen is an undulating swill of dysfunction, oozing uncontrollably and taking unpredictable dramatic shape. This is the primordial genetic swamp from which all manner of modern neuroses arise and into which *Punch-Drunk Love* slides.

Barry Egan (Sandler) is about as anxious a person you'd want to find. Berated since childhood by a gaggle of seven insensitive sisters who never listen to him, Barry is so divorced from familial, social and personal contact that his emotional emptiness shapes Sherman Oaks into a desolate terrain of terrifying width and infinite vacuousness. Yet within this oppressive psychological landscape, Barry appears pathetic, laughable, dismissable – until one experiences the raging storm within him. These moments are violently conveyed by some of the most devastating sonar-shock effects recorded in cinema (such as the opening car crash); visually intensified by his isolated and caged panic attacks (such as the heavily distorted restaurant bathroom demolition); and vocally displayed by his capacity to scream into phones with the force of interstate tornadoes (such as his yelling match with Dean [Hoffman]). Switching violently between states of control and disability, Barry is always reverberating with his alternate state – literally disconnected as he grimly clasps ripped phones following his rupturing encounters with those who pressure him into deepening psychosis.

Punch-Drunk Love is delicately and finely constructed of the minutiae which comprise Barry's world. True to the aural reality of panic attacks, psychotic episodes and anxiety disorders, sound is received in pre-amplified, over-compressed and highly distorted fragments which stretch one's emotional dynamic range. This leads to psychological exhaustion, due to a debilitating aural fatigue: everyone's voices become irritatingly

Punch-Drunk Love: true to the aural reality of panic attacks

loud; tones of their delivery become perceptually congested. The overall presence of sound in *Punch-Drunk Love* is designed and mixed to simulate this impossibly broadened dynamic range where sounds either detonate or tickle. Respite and solace are found in numerous touches of beautifully subtle sonics: from gentle hums when freezer doors are opened, to rattling of unseen debris in deserted streets.

Punch-Drunk Love's score is a chemical read-out of Barry's fluctuations and imbalances. It therapeutically wraps itself around him like a much-needed hug in decorous waltzes which conduct a lost world of idyllic bonding as he is drawn towards the honesty and openness of Lena (Watson). It diagnostically breaks out from within his boiling psyche in passages of multi-tracked percussive improvisations – not on but completely around a drum kit, like the kit itself is quaking in paranormal response to Barry's inner turmoil. If love is about losing control and 'falling in', *Punch-Drunk Love* is certainly a love story. But the film is in fact an inversion of that archaic and ultimately false 'punch-drunk' manifestation of the heart. The unfashionable love which wells up in *Punch-Drunk Love* is a calming, stabilising and welcome psychoacoustic Prozac: those who hear it swear by it.

Dir: Paul Thomas Anderson; **Prod:** Paul Thomas Anderson, Daniel Lupi, Joanne Sellar; **Scr:** Paul Thomas Anderson; **DOP:** Robert Elswit; **Editor:** Leslie Jones; **Score:** John Brion; **Sound Design:** Christopher Scarabosio, Gary Rydstrom; **Main Cast:** Adam Sandler, Emily Watson, Philip Seymour Hoffman, Luis Guzman.

Querelle
US, 1982 – 120 mins
Rainer Werner Fassbinder

Querelle tries very hard to be erotic. In a purgatory seaport of an invented Brest where its sailors, officers, guards, bartenders, whores, singers, police and masons seem trapped in self-flagellating circles of desire and repression, fucking is on everyone's lips. The dialect of this dead zone is sex itself, where everyone voices the unspoken, the unsayable, the unrepeatable. Voice therefore occupies a specific place in *Querelle*, as it is the signification of transgressive acts – due to the film being based on an imagined and canonised life of writer Jean Genet. Just as *Querelle*'s architecture and its interiors are clear manifestations of what would normally be latent libidinal form, its edge-of-the-world realm is a total inversion of the repressed heterosexual surfaces of a hysterically male dimension. A homosexual thickness covers all, and the incessantly hard and cold talk of cocks and arseholes is dramatically and symbolically framed by its utterance.

Yet for all the power voice holds in *Querelle*, its dead recording and flat delivery posits it as key factor in the film's vociferous asexuality. Lush sets, gorgeous colours, beautiful bodies and sculptural faces picture the seaport as an ideal vision of beauty iconicised by Genet's sexual imagination. But every time Querelle (Davis) taunts and tackles those around him, bartender Nono (Kaufmann) declares his power and control over others, and Lieutenant Seblon (Nero) warbles onanistically into his Dictaphone, their words dry up despite their transgressive allure and poetic warmth. Ambiguous as befits the film's post-modern flirtatiousness, this act of theatrical negation could be purposeful: its sonic veneer recalls the cheapest of porno films from the 70s (gay, straight and all that becomes the sliding between them). In the Genet ethos, that would equate to pissoir graffiti. The blunt, ugly obviousness of the hard core can be a popper for those wishing to bypass *amour*. *Querelle*'s vocalisation is definitely of this type.

Music in *Querelle* – the glimmer of breath beyond the voices' drained projection – is strangely repressed. A short fragment of male vocal glories sensuously builds upon a rich monochordal drone. Capable of imbuing the film with an emotional and sexual depth beyond its flaunted visual flatness, it is repeated endlessly and in isolated recall like a pornographic film loop. Its richness is contrasted to the distracted barroom combo-tinkling, the irrational surges of melodramatic orchestration, and the sexually drained chanson of Lysiane (Moreau) intoning 'each man kills the things he loves'. The episodic placement of these latter themes ensures that *Querelle* remains a thoroughly anxious text, ultimately desperate and dateless in its hand-wringing melodrama. Ironically, one of the few arousing moments occurs when Querelle kisses Gil (Psschl) on the mouth in silence – recalling the most open of sexual directives: shut up and make love to me.

Dir: Rainer Werner Fassbinder; **Prod:** Dieter Schidor; **Scr:** Burkhard Driest, Rainer Werner Fassbinder; **DOP:** Xaver Schwarzenberger, Josef Vavra; **Editor:** Rainer Werner Fassbinder, Juliane Lorenz; **Score:** Peer Raben; **Sound:** Hartmut Eichgron, Vladimir Vizner; **Main Cast:** Brad Davis, Franco Nero, Jeanne Moreau, Laurent Malet, Hanno Psschl, Günther Kaufmann.

Resident Evil
Germany, 2002 – 100 mins
Paul W. S. Anderson

While the modernist programme of cinema has explored ways to shatter forms inherited by linear and causal storytelling models, cinema's post-modern programme has had to navigate a terrain strewn with pre-exploded, de-diagramaticised and post-operated modules. In too many instances, the post-modern impulse has tended towards simply putting the pieces back together, creating assemblages whose sealing of cracks and erasing of fractures are deigned to be radical reinventions of narrative.

Into this smoothed-over world comes *Resident Evil*. Knowingly born of the modernist rubble that gave cinema its noise, it overrides both the desire to shatter and the urge to repair. In place, it proposes a narrative form, momentum and purpose derived from interactivity and dictated by multiplicity. Based around the cartographic spread of its originating PlayStation game, *Resident Evil* makes no attempt to translate the horizontal maze of its navigational gameplay into a vertical articulation of dramatic shape. Its 'story' is less a brace of events (via scriptwriting) or a set of objectives (via interactive authoring) and more a spatio-temporal trap in which the audience is subjected to audiovisual stress. In effect, you neither watch *Resident Evil* nor play it: for its duration, you are played.

Resident Evil's audiovision is deliberately aimed at the viewer/auditor. The most noticeable aspect of its soundtrack is the dissolution between score, song, atmosphere, sound effect and Foley effects. All are molecularly merged not in the name of Frankensteinian monstrousness, but in a far more grotesque form of sono-plastic surgery. An excess of aural detailing has no corresponding analogue to the on-screen visuals, while conventions of accompaniment and synchronism to on-screen visuals are withheld, suppressed and tortured into new and ungainly configurations. As the film's desperate band of soldiers charge through the underground research facility whose central computer system has shut down to contain a deadly airborne virus, creaks, bangs, clangs, draughts, rattles and rumbles will all, in compressed spans of screen time, shift from being musical suggestion to aural sublimation to sonic assault. Ultimately, the soundtrack is neural in design: all is generated to increase adrenaline and focus one on a singular drive – to escape and survive. Character, plot, theme and subtext vaporise in the nervous sweat and anxious panting the film induces from its audience.

Much of what is sited at the nexus of cinema and post-modernism is tragically backward, from simulative technologies that ape historically overcoded discourses of illusion, to interactive paradigms that narrow reader options more than they broaden or multiply them. Nowhere is this more apparent than in the contemporary film soundtrack, where the armoury of sonically simulative technological processes – orchestral samples, ambisonic microphones, digital spatialisation, time-code accuracy, automated mixing – are usually at the pathetic service of the most banal imaginations. *Resident Evil* is a lodged, viral anti-matter striking at the heart of cinema's classical, modern and post-modern palpitations. Partially a soundtrack; mostly a noise attack.

Dir: Paul W. S. Anderson; **Prod:** Paul W. S. Anderson, Jeremy Bolt, Bernd Eichinger, Samuel Hadida; **Scr:** Paul W. S. Anderson; **DOP:** David Johnson; **Editor:** Alexander Berner; **Score:** Marco Baltrami, Marilyn Manson; **Sound Design:** Stefan Busch, Nigel Holland; **Special Sound Effects Synthesis:** John Jackson, Buck Sanders, Dennis Smith; **Main Cast:** Milla Jovovich, Ryan McCluskey, Oscar Pearce, Indra Ové, Heike Makatsch, Eric Mabius.

Rosetta
Belgium, 1999 – 95 mins
Jean-Pierre Dardenne, Luc Dardenne

The sound of breath is the most ignored phoneme of our existence, yet its most vital siren. In *Rosetta*, the breath of a desperate girl becomes a raging ocean of white noise. Rosetta (Dequenne) generates what is possibly the most felt presence of any performer in the history of cinema due to her breath. As she frantically yet with frightening determination fights for the most menial of jobs, she becomes life itself: a throbbing, pulsating orb of climatic circularity. Drenched in feverish moisture, expelling clouds of mist in the cold, her body is reduced to temperature, momentum, change.

Working against the grain of art-house depictions of young women, *Rosetta* refuses eroticism with as much conviction as Rosetta seeks work. Rather than wish to possess her body – the prepared impulse of erotic cinema – we perceive its vitality. As she races across outer suburban fringes where droning freeways adjoin disused farmlands, the camera hugs near to her, darting after her like news cameras in a war zone: Rosetta is battling for her life. We become her lungs, heaving in palpitations as her waves of anxiety affect one in respiratory entrainment.

Folded into the vast depths of her anxiety are her menstrual cramps whose timing and intensity attack her like a vaporous poltergeist. Holed up in the cramped confines of the caravan she shares with her alcoholic mother (Yernaux), she rips clothes away from her abdomen and blasts herself with a hair dryer. The banal privacy of these scenes with their rushing noise drowning out her gasps of pain are a universe away from the genteel voyeurism which presents virginal beauty as some unearthly embodiment of pulchritude, framed in the deathly silence of water colours or soft-focus photography. *Rosetta* paints youth as a screaming record of bodily crisis, blocking any pleasure to be gained from its exposure.

Rosetta: youth as a screaming record of bodily crisis

Rosetta lives her life as a sign of her own corporeality, projected by her cries, coughs, groans, sniffles, screams. Not an animal, but an excess of humanity – one that goes beyond the encodable threshold of that which is allowed by cinema's representation of the actor. If you only had to hug one person, it would be Rosetta. That is what her only potential friend in the world, Riquet (Rongione), moves towards. And at that very moment, the film ends; cutting to black with the most deafening silence that proclaims Rosetta lives.

Dir: Jean-Pierre Dardenne, Luc Dardenne; **Prod:** Jean-Pierre Dardenne, Luc Dardenne, Laurent Pétin, Michèle Pétin; **Scr:** Jean-Pierre Dardenne, Luc Dardenne; **DOP:** Alain Marcoen; **Editor:** Marie-Hélène Dozo; **Score:** Jean-Pierre Cocco; **Sound:** Jeanne-Pierre Duret, Thomas Gauder; **Main Cast:** Émilie Dequenne, Fabrizio Rongione, Anne Yernaux.

Rumble Fish
US, 1983 – 94 mins
Francis Ford Coppola

Teens and their environment: is the trouble within their being, or their being where they are? The score to *Rumble Fish* makes no attempt to distinguish between the psychological and the social. Matching the film's rigorous meld of set and location, available light and staged fluorescence, the score percolates with contorting melodic lines, spasmodic key changes and teasing rhythmic shapes, played on a range of recognisable instruments but meshed with billiard-ball cracking, freight-train chugging, typewriter clacking, spring-clock ticking and oil-well pumping.

Painting an interior landscape within which the film's teens are staged, the score avoids all recourse to plaster music of their consumptive mode across the soundtrack (the kind proffered by alt.com music supervisors in Hollywood since the MTV-80s). In place, *Rumble Fish* offers a highly percussive jitteriness that maps teen anxieties and tensions, adhering to beats not in obedience to rock's dogmatic blocking, but to reference the body's own eruption of hormonal pubescent palpitations. As the music attaches itself to Rusty (Dillon), his dwindling and disaffected gang, plus his enigmatic brother Motorcycle Boy (Rourke), one feels their agitation and frustration. The score takes on a bubbling alchemical quality as its densely interlocked rhythms create webs of urban noise and surging tempos which trap Rusty in an emotional gridlock.

While the film is brimful of allusion and stylistic quotation (the most famous being the choreographed fight sequence in the overpass shadows which replicates the gangs' 'dance of death' from *West Side Story*), the music remains alien and unrecognisable. Its texture and presence lean against no slight or lilting musical style, and instead are invented, imagined and created as something not fitting the visually luxurious scenes and their impressive black and white cinematography.

Deliberately alienated and alienating, the score strikes gangly poses and flits into odd-angled postures, gesturally matching Rusty and Motorcycle Boy's nervy-but-cool affectations, their vibrating and humming insecurities and their mistimed explosions and resolutions.

But the music is not all a matter of inwardly collapsing decomposition. Just as Rusty rebels irrationally against whatever rubs him the wrong way in the small claustrophobic town which entraps him and his going-nowhere gang, clock time is sounded throughout *Rumble Fish* as an imprisoning stricture. The music's hyperactive rhythms rush alongside, between and against the metronomic fascism of the fateful passing of time, keyed by the incessant images of clocks and their mechanisms throughout the film. Evoking the classroom clock which seems to go too slow and the pool hall clock which seems to go too fast, the music's expulsion is guided by these archetypal teen tempos which relate to actual time yet push against its fatalistic momentum.

Dir: Francis Ford Coppola; **Prod:** Doug Claybourne, Fred Roos; **Scr:** Francis Ford Coppola; **DOP:** Stephen H. Burum; **Editor:** Barry Malkin; **Score:** Stewart Copeland; **Sound Design:** Richard Beggs, Edward Beyer; **Main Cast:** Matt Dillon, Mickey Rourke, Diane Lane, Dennis Hopper, Diana Scarwid, Vincent Spano, Nicolas Cage, Chris Penn, Laurence Fishburne, Tom Waits.

The Samurai (Le Samouraï)
France, 1967 – 105 mins
Jean-Pierre Melville

The Samurai is a sound film about silence. Closely monitoring the cool stealth of hired killer Jeff Costello (Delon), the film employs silence to encase Jeff in a sealed zone of 'non-selfhood'. There he is a 'samurai', comfortable with never being at ease with his surroundings, and never announcing his presence to anyone.

Jeff's apartment is a negative space. Its grey walls, minimum furniture and bare essentials mark it as an uninhabited domus, like a hotel apartment waiting to be rented. Jeff lives in this void, on the cusp of possibly returning or possibly departing, ready to vacate at a moment's notice. The visual and formal emptiness of the space is sonically identified through its aural suppression. Cars pass by occasionally, but no noise of others is heard: no voices, radios, doors, bells. Nor does anything in his apartment 'sound itself': no dripping taps, fridge hums, blowing fans, electric globes.

The only sound which marks the space is his pet bird, incongruously centred in a fancy cage. The bird pulses its chirps like a living barometer, attuned to the silent emptiness Jeff has specifically created for himself. Jeff never speaks in this space – maybe occasionally to make a cryptic phone call. When he is there, he is invisible. Over the opening titles, a long static camera shot depicts the space in high-contrast early morning light. The bird intermittently chirps like one's breathing cycles; Jeff is only detectable from rhythmically intermittent swirls of smoke which rise from his subsumed dark form lying on the bed.

Jeff's job is to be similarly silent and invisible. He is hired by intermediaries representing agents of whom Jeff wishes to know nothing. His taciturn exchanges are severely reduced to bare communication. He makes himself invisible within the public zones where he carries out a contract. He says little if anything to his

The Samurai: a sound film about silence

victims prior to silencing those who must be erased. When he is double-crossed, his controlled world of silence, disappearance and withdrawal starts not to crumble, but to build itself into a case for the police and a problem for those who thought they could do away with him.

After he becomes a major suspect in a hit – despite a key witness, Valerie (Rosier), remaining silent when prompted to identify him – the police bug his apartment. Two detectives place the device in total silence. Throughout their activity, the bird becomes fretful: it recognises a different kind of silence in its territory. When Jeff returns, he instantly notices that the chirping rhythm of the bird is different, and is alerted to his space having been transgressed. As the police close in on him, his presence becomes noted more and more. Realising that he has now become identifiable, recognisable and discernible, his mission of self-erasure has failed – as has his sense of 'non-selfhood'. Once made form, he commits ritual suicide – by attempting to kill his next victim with empty bullets, knowing that the police will silence him in this act.

Dir: Jean-Pierre Melville; **Prod:** Raymond Borderie; **Script:** Jean-Pierre Melville, Georges Pellegrin; **DOP:** Henri Decaë; **Editor:** Monique Bonnot, Yo Maurette; **Score:** François de Roubaix; **Sound Editor:** Robert Pouret; **Main Cast:** Alain Delon, François Périer, Nathalie Delon, Cathy Rosier.

Satyricon
Italy, 1969 – 138 mins
Federico Fellini

Where does *Satyricon* take place? Not figuratively, but actually. The social urb that harbours Encolpio's (Potter) residence early in the story is a strange construction. A maze of stacked caves rendered as the negative space around a ziggurat, its deep central shaft is an acoustic Tower of Babel, amplifying and echoing all the freaks who inhabit the pocks and nooks of its spiralled walls. In this abominable apartment block, space is insinuated; scale is denied; linkage is disallowed; proximity is negated.

The sonorum of *Satyricon*'s soundtrack is synchronised to the decivilised compression and barbaric explosion of space which entraps these cave-dwellers. The noise of the crowd, the voice of the populace, even the sound of the city – all reach monstrous levels in its cacophonic brew of oration, quotation and declamation. Music – the manifestation of social intercourse in the aural domain – consequently becomes a roaring ruckus which climaxes with the apocalyptic collapse of this volcanic urb.

The heavy irony of *Satyricon* – at times thematised, at others theatricalised – is focused on the collapse of civilisation and the swelling rise of Roman decadence over Greek enlightenment. While bodies are fixated upon for their gaudy glamour which cannot hide sweating skin, the overlapping of multiple musical voices is presented as evidence of the collapse of communication. Modern electro-acoustic sounds fuse with archaic rituals; fragments of Tibetan, Indonesian and African music evoke a polyglot slave market. No one voice reigns; no continuity organises their flow and development.

The peak of decadence is sited at Trimalcione's (Romagnoli) banquet, not simply through the vile gluttony and bitter comedy which criss-cross the camera's arcs over steaming chimeras of gastronomical form, but through the hysterical fluctuations of theatrical space. Poems, songs, dances, scenarios are suddenly born and killed in the noisy exchange of the banquet's gathering. Some stare at the camera; others are framed with their own spotlights; some become background detailing; others are irrationally highlighted only to be passed over. Speech and music contest each other and themselves in gladiatorial battle under the bemused and pompous gaze of Trimalcione – one of many figures in *Satyricon* enthralled by the sound of his own voice. Meanwhile, the voice of 'true' poetry – the Greek-quoting Eumolpo (Randone) is met with projectiles of food.

Silence coincides with the suicide of the most unfitting apparition in the film: a sophisticated humane family. With Caesar toppled, they know they will be next. Their pastel domus becomes a softened tomb once they free their slaves with dignity and send off their children so as to take their life with calm reserve. Yet this is a strange and somewhat forced detour in *Satyricon*, for the film does not bemoan the fall of the Roman Empire. In fact *Satyricon* celebrates the thick horizontal spread of its uniquely Italian debauchery by intensifying the most potent signs of its verticality – not in the construction of great monuments, but in an ever-rising volume of noise.

Dir: Federico Fellini; **Prod:** Alberto Grimaldi; **Scr:** Federico Fellini, Brunello Rondi, Bernadino Zapponi; **DOP:** Giuseppe Rotunno; **Editor:** Ruggero Mastroianni; **Score:** Nina Rota; **Sourced Score:** Ilhan Mimaroglu, Tod Dockstader, Andrew Rudin; **Sound:** Oscar De Arcangelis; **Main Cast:** Martin Potter, Hiram Keller, Max Born, Salvo Randone, Mario Romagnoli, Capucine.

Scarface
US, 1983 – 163 mins
Brian De Palma

Inside the head of Tony Montana (Pacino) is a disco. A complete club, decked out with roving lights, bass bins, mirrored walls, velour couches and marble ashtrays. That club is *Scarface*. Mistaken as a film, it is a noise-filled, cocaine-addled, booming Babylonian bathroom of decadent decline, where the American dream shares a jacuzzi with the Cuban nightmare. With all subtlety checked at the front door, *Scarface*'s grossness is maintained and monitored by that most maligned musical genre: disco. The film's defiant employment of a disco song score further ostracises it from just about every existing ideology which dictates what does not qualify as 'film music'.

But disco is the film's power. It is it's throbbing cock, its Latino machismo, its enflamed nasal passages. It is the aural embodiment of power's surge within the body, be it erotic or narcotic, personal or financial, official or criminal. Hedonistic, unrelenting, annihilating, disco in *Scarface* is the Latin lover come to deflower all that is white and genetically pure in America. Declaimed for its mulatto Otherness and sexual excess, it strikes terror into the musical heartland that proposes America's musicological heritage comes from its colonisation alone – that any musical deviations from, say, rock's enslavement of the blues must be an invasion, an infection, an incursion. Yet disco is still (unbelievably) treated like the Cuban refugees in *Scarface*: both are to be interred as they signal the flood from the other side, ready to take over. In one of the few generous musicological allowances in American cinema, *Scarface* opens the floodgates onto its soundtrack, drowning it with string-synthesisers that soar like painted skies and programmed drum machines that rattle like automatic money-counters.

Critically debased by cinema's moralists, *Scarface* deliberately wallows in its flaunted political incorrectness, dives into coke-laden tables, and bathes upon its blood-drenched staircases. To presume that the film is doing anything but 'getting high on its own supply' is to misread its self-abusing and self-destructive purpose. Unlike the silver-haired and -spooned white Miami upper class which bristles at the sight of Cuban bad guys in tuxedos, *Scarface* neither judges its eponymous character, nor disavows his Latino lineage. Talk of pussy, tongues and balls performs like someone unexpectedly putting their wet tongue in your ear; images of perspex seats, photo-landscape wallpaper and custom neon signs are held up not for ridicule but to be celebrated as warranted displays of empowerment and attainment. Staged and choreographed as a form of grotesque Italian opera, the film's audiovisual excess is as direct and pure as an uncut mound of cocaine on a black marble table. Undiluted, unrefined, unprocessed, *Scarface* is cinema transformed into disco, tracking Tony Montana as he is both dehumanised and personified as power.

Dir: Brian De Palma; **Prod:** Martin Bregman; **Scr:** Oliver Stone; **DOP:** John A. Alonzo; **Editor:** Gerald B. Greenberg, David Ray; **Score:** Giorgio Moroder; **Supervising Sound Editor:** Edward Beyer; **Main Cast:** Al Pacino, Steven Bauer, Michelle Pfeiffer, Mary Elizabeth Mastrantonio, Robert Loggia, F. Murray Abraham.

Scorpio Rising
US, 1968 – 30 mins
Kenneth Anger

Just as Charles Manson claimed to have envisioned a racial apocalypse in the Beatles' 'Helter Skelter', *Scorpio Rising* invites one to consider mystical and psycho-sexual possibilities in the Crystals' 'He's A Rebel', the Vandellas' 'Heatwave' and the Angels' 'My Boyfriend's Back'. These and other supposedly innocuous 60s pop songs colonise the film's soundtrack, running parallel to the bricolage of images worshipping motorcycle boy culture. Spooled like a silent film with a disconnected radio broadcast, *Scorpio Rising* uses synchronicity and fortuitous circumstance to fatally tie sound and image together as part of a faux-cosmological treatise on 'the other side'.

Corny and syrupy on the one hand yet entirely beguiling on the other, the film's surface trappings, mauled icons and fetishised trinkets ultimately dress its meaning in drag. Sexual duality is celebrated as the film's correlation between sound and image becomes less a fixture of contrast and more an act of becoming. The film ventures into a pre-queer sub-gay homosexuality that clothes clandestine sexuality in mysterious ritual: lone pouting boys in their narcissistic bedrooms grooming themselves and preparing their night attire; insolent grease monkeys in their Frankensteinian 'workshop of filthy creation', assembling devilish chrome machines; gatherings of outdoor zooming bikers and indoor revelling studs – all are suggestively engaged in foreplay, arousal and satiation as Ricky Nelson describes his 'Teenage Idol' and Bobby Vinton yearns for 'Blue Velvet'.

Not in the least concerned with outward declaration, *Scorpio Rising* thrills to the hidden, wherein suppression works to masochistically enflame one's knowing of that which hides in the light. Evoking the erotic Morse code of Jean Genet, tokens and totems of the clean and youthful side of 60s biker culture are underlaid with exciting significance. The film's images turn the song-worlds upside down to read that which has been covertly inscribed underneath their labelling, exposing a universe of transgressive desire. *Scorpio Rising* progressively shrinks the distance between an innocent youth straddling his bike outside a carnival at the weekend, and a decadent biker urinating into his helmet while standing on a church altar. (Pseudo-subliminal flash frames of an erect penis, whipped buttocks and bulging crotches also spike the film's party punch.)

Evolving into an apocalyptic debauchery of speed, leather, skin, lights and smoke, *Scorpio Rising* grows dark as its figures are lost in black voids, barely lit apart from their protruding form. Signalled by visions of Hitler, Jesus and Brando, plus the spiralling dissension of songs like Gene McDaniels's 'Point of No Return' and the Surfari's 'Wipe Out', *Scorpio Rising*'s boy idols attain transcendental states of objectification, as their faces and beings become obliterated by their costumery. Demonic sonic swirls of roaring engines, screaming gangs, squealing pigs and clinking chains crowd the soundtrack as the images become more abstract. Finally, the film passes over into a wider, totalising necromantic domain, carrying with it the risen scorpions it has cinematically conjured forth.

Dir: Kenneth Anger; **Prod:** Kenneth Anger; **Scr:** Kenneth Anger; **DOP:** Kenneth Anger; **Editor:** Kenneth Anger; **Sourced Songs:** Ricky Nelson, Bobby Vinton, Gene McDaniels, the Surfaris, the Vandellas, the Angels, Kris Jensen, Little Peggy March, Ray Charles, Elvis Presley, Claudine March; **Main Cast:** Bruce Byron.

Seduced and Abandoned (Sedotta e abbandonata)
Italy, 1964 – 115 mins
Pietro Germi

Italian pop music from the mid-50s to the late 60s has the most distinctive reverberant quality of any recorded music. Hyper-compressed, its spatial congestion is so powerful its resonance alchemically takes form, covering the voice like a solid fatty mass. This robust thickening is a technological simulation of the hearty corporeal vim of Italian culture, where flavours, recipes and bowel movements merge with every facet of life.

What sounds like an outlandish string of metaphors is held under your nose in *Seduced and Abandoned*, a savage parody of family values and 'matters of honour' Calabrese-style. An absurdly melodramatic baritone *canzona* bellows over shots of the Ascalone women making their way to church. They traipse the town's dusty steps, the song swirling around their black asexual mourning attire which attempts to hide their womanhood from the world. This sets up a repeated and grand tradition lambasted by the film: women as virginal figurines which men pathologically desire to become whores and harlots. The soundtrack's song salaciously attempts to seduce the women; the social outcome will be that they are abandoned.

Back home after the Sunday dinner, young Agnese (Sandrelli) continues her study while the rest of the family partake of their post-repast siesta. The camera tracks across their bloated, sweating bodies as they snore; flies buzz around the kitchen leftovers; outside, the soft but omnipresent song-calls of hawkers float across the town's midday quiet. Although the rather repulsive Peppino (Puglisi) is engaged to Agnese's sister, he lusts after Agnese, pushing her into the kitchen and sexually overpowering her. As she falls into his arms, church organ music wells up: jump-cut to her breathless confession in church as a priest hoarsely harangues her into Catholic self-loathing.

Seduced and Abandoned: aural obesity and the *canzona* tradition

Before long, her pregnancy is discovered, and the patriarch of the family – Don Vincenzo (Urzì) – becomes the enraged amplifier of 'family principles', screaming at the top of his voice throughout the household and in a variety of public spaces. He broadcasts his family ethics to the town like a distorted loudspeaker, typifying the potent oral tradition of social discourse in Italian culture (the writing credits of the film list four authors, all for scripting dialogue). Contrasted against this is Agnese's silence: her initial withdrawal from the family dynamic as she mouths her penance; her refusal to speak up and name Peppino; her imprisonment in her bedroom where she can speak to no one.

As matters get hysterically out of hand, Don Vincenzo and Agnese each have a nightmarish vision of Agnese's marriage to Peppino. Combined with grotesque camera work is the same reverberant texture evocative of the film's phonological *canzona*. At other times, radios and fragments of score detonate their wall-of-sound onto the soundtrack, never underscoring and always obliterating the action like a deafening Caruso. When Peppino comes to serenade Agnese in one of the many convoluted inter-familial strategies to right his wrongs, he is accompanied by the town mortician who has designed battery-powered speakers for his guitar: this results in Peppino's voice wafting through the streets with the same aural obesity of all recorded music in the film. The film closes on the marble bust of the departed Don Vincenzo as a flatulent brass band pumps and wheezes and we read his epitaph: 'Family and Honour'.

Dir: Pietro Germi; **Prod:** Franco Cristaldi, Luigi Giacosi; **Scr:** Pietro Germi; **DOP:** Aiace Parolin; **Editor:** Roberto Cinquini; **Score:** Carlo Rustichelli; **Songs:** Guido Nardone; **Sound:** V. Biraschi, F. Bassi; **Main Cast:** Stefania Sandrelli, Saro Urzì, Aldo Puglisi, Lando Buzzanca, Oreste Palella.

Shaft
US, 1971 – 100 mins
Gordon Parks Jr

Some may find it hard to listen to the score to *Shaft* devoid of the retro-revisionist parodies based on the iconography the score so perfectly stylised. Contrary to the presumption that the score is no more than a rattling background as performed by a TV show session band trying to be funky, it is a vital musicological document that embodies many of the blues, jazz and R&B traits which had been progressively seeping into American crime film music for the preceding fifteen years.

For all the corniness attributed to its excessive flourishes, *Shaft*'s score withholds some intricate semiological cross-referencing. Its famous hi-hats and wah-wah guitar perfectly portray a predominant black figure in American cinema: the man on the run. Trailing all the way back to escaped slaves, this breathless, manic being populates blues references of hopping freight trains and jazz interpretations of taking flight and escaping one's confines. The vowelled jostling of this musical effect throughout most of *Shaft*'s themes distils it to a tantalising electronic gesture via the prominent use of the wah-wah fuzz pedal – arguably brought to a boiling point by Jimi Hendrix. In *Shaft*, it streams across shots of urban streets and intersections to such an extent that the music evokes a mapped grid of the city as it is traversed by private detective John Shaft (Rowntree). A subtle but political undercurrent is also expressed by the film's dramatic depiction of a black man not on the run, but running after others. Shaft is both hunter and game in this urban jungle, so the music's breathless panting is part anxiety but part thrill.

The flutes, trombones, hi-hats, guitars and piano of *Shaft* define and enshrine the explosive sound of the black city that is blaxploitation: a rapaciously anti-white world imaged by and predicated on a black experience of the collapsed metropolis which no Mr-Brady-in-a-frizz-hairdo could architecturally set right. But this isn't the spooky black-of-night where noir meets crime in the meld of pulp fiction. The domain of blaxploitation is brightly lit, loudly coloured, sharply focused and garishly situated. Clothes are vulgar, dialogue is grotesque, comedy is offensive, sex is delicious, speed is noisy, guns are desirable, drugs are food, money is oxygen. Visually, *Shaft* is more casual documentary than colourful bombast. But the music is so 'black' – so thickly funky and sexually potent – that it is hard to find a more aggressive period in the history of film scores as that unleashed by the distinctiveness of *Shaft*. The excessiveness of its audiovisual carnival is a jubilant celebration of image being returned to sound – imagery which Hollywood had commenced suppressing in the 20s in its whiting-out of black presence and power. Blaxploitation movies carry the intensity of this blackness in high detail and sharp relief, shining like ebony under arc lights, ignited by the chants of 'Burn, Hollywood! Burn!' The score to *Shaft* plays loudly underneath, over and on top, encapsulating an urban musical culture projected through the dark prism of blaxploitation in all its defiant and pointed irresponsibility.

Dir: Gordon Parks Jr; **Prod:** Joel Freeman; **Script:** Ernest Tidyman, John D. F. Black; **DOP:** Urs Furrer; **Editor:** Hugh A. Robertson; **Score and Songs:** Issac Hayes; **Sound:** Lee Bost, Hal Watkins; **Main Cast:** Richard Rowntree, Moses Gunn, Charles Cioffi, Christopher St John, Gwenn Mitchell, Lawrence Pressman.

The Shining
UK, 1980 – 115 mins
Stanley Kubrick

The resolutely atonal score to *Psycho* has propelled a network of spindly shards and knots through numerous 'psycho' movies since. A knowing revision of its contribution to musical psychosis is found in the selection of music for *The Shining* – in particular, the excerpts from Krzysztof Penderecki's *De Natura Sonoris No. 2* and *Polymorphia*, Béla Bartók's *Music for Strings, Percussion and Celesta*, and György Ligeti's *Lontano*. Collectively and individually they celebrate the abject violence of Nature in all its cosmological eventfulness. While fantasy and horror colour the story of Jack Torrance (Nicholson) gradually being possessed by ghosts in the hotel he manages during the winter close-down, the music's overall presence and purpose in *The Shining* is to posit a numbing humanist grounding which suggests Jack's psychosis is not supernatural but simply natural.

The Shining's tactical incorporation of the orchestra is canny. Certainly the orchestra has for at least three centuries used its mass and size to create intimidating landscapes, portraits, visions and journeys which evoke the scale of Nature's destructive, creative and rejuvenating powers. But Penderecki's archly modernist post-war decimation of harmonic fixture encodes the sonic detailing of the destruction of the orchestra itself – overtly signified by the aggressive scraping of the string section. Through his direction of performer technique, Penderecki works beyond abstraction to a pure material essence as he forces the players of his score to rip open that polished wood detailing on the violin and expose the shrieking soul trapped in its casing.

As Jack creeps up the stairs swinging a baseball bat at his wife Wendy (Duvall), Penderecki's strings slice the air like deadly bursts of steam expelled through Jack's flaring nostrils. Elsewhere, during unsettling moments where Danny (Lloyd) has visions of the hotel's bloody past and Jack is slipping further into the hotel's ghost world, the orchestra rumbles like a needle left in a Deutsche Grammophon disc while a mild earth tremor vibrates the diamond stylus. Most importantly, *The Shining* eschews 'cues' in favour for asynchronous passages which extemporise the narrative and sculpt a dramatic ambience wherein a character's psychosis becomes an aura which taints, tinges and terrifies all other existence in its space. Just as *Psycho*'s score charts the surges in Norman's emotional instability, Penderecki's passages in particular function as a soundtrack to the core synaptic overloads which induce psychosis. In the film's placement of these passages, 'scoring' follows neural and metabolic arcs of Jack, Wendy and Danny's terror, instead of syncing disharmony to match the sudden appearance of spooks and bogey-men.

While clouds of atonality hiss and steam, chiming with the psychological friction and fissuring which slowly crack Jack, other musical gestures relate more to the decayed corporeality of the dead zone which beckons him. Memorable moments of repulsion occur when Jack comes into contact with this – usually through febrile instances triggered by taste, smell and touch. Bartók's intricate transpositions of insect harmonics and frequencies generate a fetid, corpulent richness which laterally and beautifully slides into the rank and rotting world of the matter that defines the presence of the dead (when Jack embraces the decrepit body of the woman from the bath). Ligeti's thickened swell of organific tones and bass-heavy drones evokes a turgidly still swamp that welcomes the dead (as when Jack intermittently yelps in his sleep, dreaming that he will kill his family). *The Shining* could have been a film about the mind; its physically affective music never lets one forget the body that houses the mind.

Dir: Stanley Kubrick; **Prod:** Robert Fryer, Mary Lea Johnson, Stanley Kubrick, Martin Richards; **Scr:** Stanley Kubrick, Diane Johnson; **DOP:** John Alcott; **Editor:** Ray Lovejoy; **Score:** Wendy Carlos; **Sourced Score:** Krzysztof Penderecki, Béla Bartók, György Ligeti; **Sound:** Dino di Campo, Jack T. Knight, Wyn Ryder; **Main Cast:** Jack Nicholson, Shelley Duvall, Danny Lloyd, Scatman Crothers.

Some Kind of Wonderful
US, 1987 – 93 mins
Howard Deutch

The world of the teen movie – like a teenager's bedroom – is open only to those sensitive to its environs. *Some Kind of Wonderful* (a beautifully vague appellation for that great teen drug, love) is a cinematic environment of pure teen spirit. Every space, wall, room, corridor is built using teen energy; it will either repel you or welcome you inside.

In *Some Kind of Wonderful*, a pressurised love triangle releases intense emotion as formed between grease monkey Keith (Stoltz), rich girl Amanda (Thompson), and quirky outsider Watts (Masterson) whose love for Keith is invisible to him. The film's plotted surface points to the drama between Keith and Amanda, posing Watts as a side character. But true to her moniker, Watts is the energised heart of the film in profoundly sonic and musical ways. The film starts with Watts drumming in her garage, listening to pounding electro-pop on her headphones, her snare pad adorned with a huge heart. This she beats, sealed in a soundproofed zone symbolic of the reclusive domain of the teen world.

Keith is a seething though quaint ball of sexual desire, pounding away in workshops and garages, getting dirty while admiring the gleaming beauty of Amanda from afar. Yet as full as his desire is, so is it misdirected: he is unknowingly responding to the charged sexuality Watts radiates despite her churlish tomboy front. This is evident not through literary interpretation: the way the film's pop songs – often selective instrumental passages – will occupy the full spectrum of the soundtrack simulates the waves of emotional nausea and epiphanous vertigo expected of love's broadcast. And at every moment a song wells up, Watts is not too far removed from its occurrence and diffusion, continually linking her energy to Keith's. Amanda, conversely, generates naught. Even when Keith courts her at the art museum on a special date, the gentility of background music is the only repository of musical symbolism attached to her. Tellingly, Keith talks sweet nothings to her in a huge empty outdoor concert auditorium – the complete inverse of Watts' deafening solitude as she pounds out her sublimated heart beats in a desperate telegraphic pulse to deaf Keith, blinded by wrong love.

If films have a 'drive' then Watts is the driver of *Some Kind of Wonderful*. Not by coincidence does she swallow her pride and be the chauffeur on Keith and Amanda's special date. She embodies the pop song score in ways imperceptible to those trained to read film scores as composed appendages to a film's scenography. Watts is a paradigm of how music functions in the teen movie. As excessive consumer of the music which operates as its score, she sets up a feedback loop based on a balance between the harmony of her sexual energy, and the

Some Kind of Wonderful: the architecsonic realm of teen love

dissonance of her emotional anxiety. When the camera tracks in to her face as well as Keith's, the music wells to such excess that it brings down the world around them. In the teen world, everything is heightened – turned up full, drowning in itself, hysterically incapable of differentiation and distinction. *Some Kind of Wonderful* perfectly sculpts an architecsonic realm of teen love that is deafening, exhausting, oceanic.

Dir: Howard Deutch; **Prod:** John Hughes; **Scr:** John Hughes; **DOP:** Jan Keisser; **Editor:** Bud S. Smith, M. Scott Smith; **Score:** Stephen Hague, John Musser; **Sourced Songs:** Propaganda, Charlie Sexton, Pete Shelly, Duffy, Flesh for Lulu, the Jesus and Mary Chain, the Apartments, the March Violets, Lick the Tins; **Supervising Sound Editor:** Mike Dobie; **Main Cast:** Eric Stoltz, Mary Stuart Masterson, Lea Thompson, Craig Sheffer, John Ashton, Elias Koteas.

The Spirit of the Beehive (*El espíritu de la colmena*)
Spain, 1973 – 95 mins
Víctor Erice

Set in a rural Castillian outpost immediately after World War II, *Spirit of the Beehive* grows within a strange social and psychological vacuum. The outside world and its events seem far removed from the town's rolling plains of natural beauty. Trains pass through infrequently; despatched mail may never reach its origin. The film traces the effect of this remoteness on a family as its members draw individual lines of dislocation and separation. Silence, ambience and aural nuance connect the desolate township, its sprawling farmlands and the family household in a gracefully calm tone. Yet the domestic quiet betrays an underworld of unmentioned thoughts and unspoken dreams.

Fernando (Gómez) runs an apiary and appears detached from his wife, Teresa (Gimpera). She sits in the emptiness of the warm but slightly dilapidated mansion and writes letters to an unnamed love of her past. Fernando meanwhile has built a glass-boxed beehive indoors which he observes late at night, ruminating on life as viewed through this bee-prism and writing in his journal. Early in the film, their voiceovers break their sealed privacy as we audit their emotional isolation – each unknown, unobserved and unheard by their partner. However, *Spirit of the Beehive* is mostly focused on their young children, Ana (Torrent) and Isabel (Tellería). They are oblivious of their parents' verbal divorce and innocently enjoy a rich and playful life, marking the emptiness of the house with their laughter and footsteps.

After being overwhelmed by a screening of *Frankenstein* in the town hall, Ana and Isabel lie awake at night. Their faces framed as haloes outlined by lamp light, they engage in a long interpretation of the film in hushed tones. The scene draws us close to their breath, and opens us up to their querying minds and fertile imagination as they both confuse and distinguish between film and reality. Not simply 'viewed through the innocent eyes of a child', *Spirit of the Beehive* is the result of having had the children share a secret directly with us; their whispering voices are crucial in exacting this exchange. From this point on, the film's emptiness reverberates with their hushed exchanges, framing the world we see as the world they audiovisually fantasise.

The children's whispering aurally tones the film, enhanced with minimal environmental sound and supported by the score's sinuous frailty and aerated understatement. Grounded in low-key sono-musical ambience, Isabel and Ana are highly sensitive receptors of emotional energy, aural suggestion and visual impression. From placing their ears on the tracks as a steam train approaches far away, to listening down deep wells, to hearing their name called by the other in dark moonlit nights, they monitor their world with a high fidelity in proportion to their susceptible minds and emotional responsiveness.

Dir: Víctor Erice; **Prod:** Elías Querejeta; **Scr:** Víctor Erice, Ángel Fernández Santos, Francisco J. Querejeta; **DOP:** Luis Cuadrado; **Editor:** Pablo González del Amo; **Score:** Luis de Pablo; **Sound:** Luis Rodriguez; **Sound Effects:** Luis Castro, Jean Michel Sire; **Main Cast:** Fernando Fernán Gómez, Teresa Gimpera, Ana Torrent, Isabel Tellería.

Stalker
Soviet Union, 1979 – 160 mins
Andrei Tarkovsky

A terse staging controls the denouement of *Stalker*. Set at the precipice dividing hope from despair, its story follows the Stalker (Kajdanovsky) as he guides the Writer (Solonitsyn) and the Scientist (Grinko) into the Zone: part nuclear wasteland, part mystical dimension. Their journey and its undulating non-specified landmarks constitute the symbolic space across which their interactions and reflections notate the film's philosophical discourse. While the film is overly literal in many respects, *Stalker*'s staging grants an alternative route to the film's audiovisual inner depths. This is particularly notable in the camera work and its lengthy static framing bracketed by extremely slow zooms and tracks. Rarely does the camera stay fixed; one senses its momentary stillness as a pause before movement. This sets up a mild anxiety in framing: one knows there is always something beyond the frame, and that the visuals at any point will open out or become lost in a forthcoming panorama of perspectival disorientation.

Stalker's sound design sometimes obeys the stricture of allowing sound only when on-screen correlation is evident; at other times it rejects this and forwards sound which clearly emanates from a non-defined off-screen realm. But this selective use of sound when combined with the camera's decisive moments of movement articulates a psychoacoustic logic which privileges the beyond – that which we are yet to visually identify or sonically locate. The 'beyond' is geographically sited as the Zone beyond which the military patrol, and as the haunting landmarks to which the Stalker alludes as they move ever forward to the 'room' where all wishes come true.

Sound and score often merge to detail *Stalker*'s beyond. The trio's hand-car journey by rail into the Zone exemplifies this, as the camera concentrates in turn on the grim faces of the Stalker, the Writer and the Scientist while the soundtrack builds a trance-inducing rhythm from its recognisable source to an interiorised musical abstraction. More *musique concrète* than melodic suggestion, sound and score meet at poetic borders, then affix their fusion to the camera's highly architectural assignation. In a more dislocating manner, the recurring periodic intrusion of unseen freight train rumble into the Stalker's apartment seems plausible until one notices distorted classical music accompanying the rattling noise, as if an orchestral machine is passing underneath the building. In each case, music symbolises the point at which the beyond – oppressive societal force, the mysterious Zone, unstable emotional incursions – intersects the physics of a character's 'here and now'.

Inversely, the Zone's many tunnels, shafts, catacombs and caves generate physical acoustic effects which blur the distinction between processed sound effects and actual acoustic sensations: reverberant owls, echoic water drops, diffused booms and clangs are all highly evocative events while sharply conjuring up the metallica of the Zone's post-industrial debris. Physics, empiricism and rationalism are slyly attacked throughout *Stalker*, and the film's mirage of audiovisual veracity eventually dissolves to expose the psychodrama of its characters' search for meaning. While at times voiced by lengthy monologues and recited poems, the film's closing scene conveys its metaphysical bent with sonic acumen. Stalker's daughter Martha (Abramova) – a 'mutant' born after the creation of the Zone – replicates the natural subsonic train rumbling which shifts glasses on tables at the opening of the film, by now pushing one over the table's edge through paranormal control.

Dir: Andrei Tarkovsky; **Prod:** Aleksandra Demidova; **Scr:** Arkadi Strugatsky, Boris Strugatsky; **DOP:** Aleksandr Knyazhinsky; **Editor:** Lyudmila Feiginova; **Score:** Eduard Artemyev; **Sound:** V. Sharun; **Main Cast:** Aleksandr Kajdanovsky, Alisa Frejndlikh, Anatoli Solonitsyn, Nikolai Grinko, Natasha Abramova.

Stand By Me
US, 1986 – 87 mins
Rob Reiner

Stand By Me does not take its title from the Ben E. King song for mere nostalgic effect. Aurally 'using' the song rather than merely referencing or placing it, the film focuses on the interiority of the song and its emotional aura. This constitutes a contra-literary mode which cinema rarely employs despite cinema's propensity for the lyrical, the evocative and the immersive – all qualities ascribed to the evocative power of songs from another era.

This mode of narration is openly declared as forty-five-year-old Gordie (Richard Dreyfuss) sits in his pick-up, reading a newspaper headline about a man killed in a hold-up. Gordie is dumbstruck by what he has read; it has violently ruptured his present, pouring in the forgotten past when he was friends with the man – Chris – of whom he now reads. Rising from the soft countryside ambience is a delicate instrumental version of 'Stand By Me'. It is slow, measured, restrained; it drips with melancholy, yearning, loss. This is song as touched by remembrance, transforming its original energy into a distanced rendition. While Ben E. King's version throws one back into the past – to the moment of its release and effect upon young Gordie – this slowed-down reverie ushers the past into the space of the present, where mature Gordie hears things as differently as he perceives his past upon reflection.

In *Stand By Me*, song is less musicological – referencing music's social contract in the act of listening – and more diaristic and interpretative – referencing the personal relationship one forms at a juncture of listening. Melding sound design with song placement and film score, the film's music mobilises memory as song through a series of spatially rendered sites: on radios in cars, transistors carried while crossing bridges, on turntables in rooms. The acoustic quality of each space is fused with the song's emission, just as the smell of a room can

Stand By Me: the interiority of song and its emotional aura

make one recall its wallpaper. As the story of *Stand By Me* is told in flashback by Gordie, the multiple manifestations of songs 'score' his memory, on top of which his voice floats. Gordie's voice is continually coloured by the moment of awareness, as if his remembering of the past as triggered by a tragic present puts everything into perspective.

Just as Gordie's words convey this, his silence is crucial in framing his awareness. Silence is what joins young Gordie (Wheaton) with his buddies Chris (Phoenix), Teddy (Feldman) and Vern (O'Connell) when they embark on a trip to witness the body of a dead boy. Its dread mute presence marks their collective journey with an acute suppression which binds them to never tell anyone of their experience. Gordie's voiceover releases him from that which he had held within for too long; his unplanned memory of the incident now allows him to break its silence.

Nostalgia is an entirely inappropriate term to describe the narrative machinations of *Stand By Me*. Not once does one hear in Gordie's voiceover a simple 'reliving of the past'. Rather, the lyrical weaving of his voice with slivers, sheets and threads of songs from his childhood era – either acoustically diffused or thematically orchestrated – conducts an aching elegy that respects how songs of the past only ever return one to that which one has lost.

Dir: Rob Reiner; **Prod:** Bruce A. Evans, Raynold Gideon, Andrew Scheinman; **Scr:** Raynold Gideon, Bruce A. Evans; **DOP:** Thomas Del Ruth; **Editor:** Robert Leighton; **Score:** Jack Nitzsche; **Sourced Songs:** Ben E. King, the Monotones, the Chordettes, Buddy Holly, the Del Vikings, the Coasters, Jerry Lee Lewis, Shirley and Lee; **Supervising Sound Editor:** Lon Bender, Wylie Stateman; **Main Cast:** Wil Wheaton, River Phoenix, Corey Feldman, Jerry O'Connell, Gary Riley, Kiefer Sutherland, Casey Siemaszko.

The Straight Story
US, 1999 – 111 mins
David Lynch

The Straight Story foregrounds ageing as a process of the present rather than as a portrait of the past. Appropriately, Alvin Straight (Farnsworth) has aged in the back story of the film, and now engages in forward action (literally, driving forth on a ride-on lawnmower) in a cathartic attempt to deal with his ageing by achieving closure through speaking to his brother Lyle (cameoed by Stanton).

The dramatic graft which forges momentum in the film's story is the silence that hangs over the Straight brothers like an unfinished sentence. Non-speech and unfinished-speech are thematically mapped across many characters of *The Straight Story*. Rose (Spacek) is traumatised by the legal removal of her children due to her own psychological instability. Her speech patterns carry the scar of this wrenching, leaving her to speak grammatically correct sentences but in a timing which forces the flow of meaning through spurted phrases. Like Alvin, her voice is her story – not through words as written into her, but as words sounded through her. These fractured voices are contrasted against the warm blanketed tones which flow forth from the friendly family with whom Alvin stays while his ride-on lawnmower is being repaired en route.

While there are many passages of the film wherein one experiences abject silence, *The Straight Story* also exploits the digital soundtrack's capacity to move accurately between aural extremes. The mix of the film noticeably does not stay at a median of acceptable audio presence. In numerous moments one is urged to listen carefully – not because of distractions, simultaneous events or sonic density, but simply because one is at a remove from spoken action. Alvin is often presented chatting with others in one unedited shot. Long, insignificant conversation is heard at a very low level, filmed from a great distance. One manages to understand words, but at a severely reduced auditory level. *The Straight Story* provides the sonic suit within which we can experience this deafness that accompanies old age.

Imbedded in these arranged silences, one sometimes hears a monophonic textured hum. It sounds like a long-ringing reverberant patina of parts of the film's lyrical score. Yet due to the rich, fixed tonality of these harmonic sheets of soft pink noise, a discernible base key works contra-harmonically to the score's apparently whimsical cues. These tones repeatedly well up to forecast the possibility that Alvin's brother may have already died. Like an emotional tinitis, this ringing is subtle but persuasive. It is the sound of the past: lingering, lilting, longing. Alvin feels that ringing, and travels across three states not merely to reunite with his blood brother, but to hear his own voice in their shared acoustic space. It is fitting that his brother is wordless at their reunion. The silence that lolls between them at the film's finish is the end to a disturbing hum which rang ceaselessly across time and space, until physical proximity could set it to rest.

Dir: David Lynch; **Prod:** Neal Edelstein, Mary Sweeney; **Scr:** John Roach, Mary Sweeney; **DOP:** Freddie Francis; **Editor:** Mary Sweeney; **Score:** Angelo Badalamenti; **Sound Design:** David Lynch; **Main Cast:** Richard Farnsworth, Sissy Spacek, Harry Dean Stanton.

Suspiria
Italy, 1977 – 98 mins
Dario Argento

If rock music in its epochal form can be characterised as an hysterical unleashing of noise in libidinal, psychological and overall mind-bending modes, then *Suspiria* truly boasts a 'rock score'. Carved in an era when 'rock opera' was viewed as a breakthrough in theatre, *Suspiria* incorporates rock music into its narrative, allowing the music to retain its violence in ways unimaginable in any Broadway production. Operatically chiming to the unending set-pieces of graphic gore and baroque expositions of murder and mayhem, the music is typically relentless, scathing and excessive.

Suspiria's rock score confounds, compacts and confuses its audience. Matching the film's often incomprehensible machinations, the music's emotional schisms and energy peaks are ill-timed to discernible actions, disproportionate to a character's tenor, and inappropriate in tone to any scenographic outline. In fact it is the loudness with which the music always presents itself that determines an audiovisual saturation. While you are often left wondering who is killing who and why, you are likely to be overwhelmed by such voluminous statement and depiction of these acts that you are bludgeoned into accepting the 'senseless violence' on screen. There is, of course, a story at the film's heart, concerning American ballet dancer Susie Banyon (Harper) who has unwittingly stumbled into a coven of witches who run a dance academy in the Bavarian Black Forest in which she has just enrolled. Yet the set-up, staging and resolution of the dramaturgy seem to be amplifying something beyond mere plot. The music is key to this amplification, and its feverish performance and ornately conducted noise characterise the film's bizarre conflation of mystical lore with pulp fiction.

Music is thus 'sounded' more than it is composed, cued or conducted. Its presence is more abstract and abject than it is representational or expressive. Its 'rockness' is allowed to be itself rather than be coded into some bland narrational voice. From the opening credits to the arrival of Susie at the airport, the music's metre is in overdrive. No reason is given for this level of drama; no symbolic direction is provided to the story's ensuing exposition. Simply, things are evil. And each time the music starts up, you are being cued for the inevitable.

At the film's apocalyptic finale, it is as if the film has spent itself. Like a drained rock performer, it has spun into its own collapsing orbit of self-destruction. It now writhes in catatonic delirium, just as Susie exits dazed and confused from the burning academy. She half smiles, soaked in the rain again, exhausted from her delirium. The credits state: 'You have been watching SUSPIRIA'. You've been listening to it, too.

Dir: Dario Argento; **Prod:** Claudio Argento; **Scr:** Dario Argento, Daria Nicolodi; **DOP:** Luciano Tovoli; **Editor:** Franco Fraticelli; **Score:** Goblin; **Sound Effects:** Luciano Anzellotti; **Main Cast:** Jessica Harper, Udo Kier, Aida Valli, Joan Bennett.

Sympathy for the Devil (*One Plus One*)
France, 1968 – 99 mins
Jean-Luc Godard

For fans of the Rolling Stones, *Sympathy for the Devil* is a documentary of the recording of one of the group's most important songs, 'Sympathy for the Devil' – irritatingly interrupted by boring speeches by Black Panthers. For fans of the highly politicised end of the *nouvelle vague* spectrum, it espouses the Panthers' views uncompromisingly – until it cuts away to a bunch of decadent drug-fucked rock stars doodling in a recording studio.

Sympathy for the Devil is a deliberately self-rupturing musicological text – one whose gouged divisions have become wider and infected as time goes on. The collision between its two textual zones – the hedonistic abandon of the Rolling Stones and the ascetic commitment of the Black Panthers – forms a statement on music and politics which illustrates and demonstrates their uncomfortable co-option and nullification of the other. Made at the height of the Parisian student rebellion, the film creates a black hole into which social change is sucked with ugly ferocity. Yet this symbolic plughole actualises a major dynamic ignored by those who advocate change. To fully acknowledge this effect, one must perceive all that binds and repels the Stones and the Panthers.

The Stones cherished and worshipped the blues, and ritualistically adorned themselves – their sound, their posture, their performance – with its musical mojos. Far from usurping the blues, the Stones' legacy is one of preventing the blues' darkened waves and spirals from being submerged by musical histories that at the time were actively segregating 'race' music from the supposedly purer and higher forms white America championed. There is no denying the socio-political effect of the Stones' blind love for black music. Conversely, the Panthers perceived the blues as the result of racial oppression and colonisation – an expression born of torturous conditions and social disenfranchisement. Being homeless and penniless signified no romantic freedom to politicised African Americans,

Sympathy for the Devil: a deliberately self-rupturing musicological text

but a new form of displaced entrapment born of 'freed slaves' left with no place in a post-Abolition era. The Stones' identified with the hoarse, ravaged and beaten tonality of both acoustic and electric blues; the Panthers preferred the socially galvanising force of African congas as a mantra to rise up and take over the new oppressors.

The divide between the two is as wide as one between parent and teenager, but the lazy mutated rhetoric of youth, music and politics has been allowed to somehow bind these conflicting cultural perspectives. Yet *Sympathy for the Devil*'s depiction of environments for each group is crucial in articulating this separation. The camera encircles the Stones in their technological 'garden of delights' as they onanistically excite themselves with their music and faux-voodoo 'woo-woos', all within the subdivided isolation of the recording studio. We witness and audition their disorganised and slovenly methods as we play in our own heads the song as a meta-text to frame the growing audiovisual assemblage of what we know has already come to be recorded. The same camera tracks past Panthers dotted throughout the splayed bowels of a techno Hades: a car junkyard strewn with the dead machina from one of American's primary industries. The Panthers' polemics and prophesies are read out from politically fundamental texts. Despite the location noise which engulfs them, they remain respectful of the words, treating them as manuals for a society which we know has not already come to be enacted.

Dir: Jean-Luc Godard; **Prod:** Eleni Collard, Michael Pearson, Iain Quarrier; **Scr:** Jean-Luc Godard; **DOP:** Colin Corby, Anthony B. Richmond; **Editor:** Agnès Guillemot, Ken Rowles; **Song:** The Rolling Stones; **Sound:** Arthur Bradburn; **Main Cast:** Mick Jagger, Keith Richards, Brian Jones, Bill Wyman, Charlie Watts, Marianne Faithfull, Anita Pallenberg, Clifton Jones, Danny Daniels, Frankie Dymon.

Talk Radio
US, 1988 – 110 mins
Oliver Stone

Audience's initial impression in 1919 of voices on the radio likened them to spirits and ghosts speaking from the beyond. The presence of a voice in one's shared acoustic space minus its face and body attributed a phantasmagorical aura to the medium of radio. *Talk Radio* superficially appears to be a realist text coded with an array of topical and societal concerns, but its sound design connects it back to a mysticism born of radio's sonic apparition.

Barry Champlain (Bogosian) is a blunt, aggressive talk radio host, maniacally fielding callers, feeding off their ignorance and feeding into their prejudices. The feedback of live talk radio is his perfect medium. *Talk Radio* methodically creates a radiophonic space for Barry's world and his voice (the two are interchangeable), a space where production design and camera work are actively engaged in 'listening to' the film's sound design.

Barry's control booth evidences this starkly. Set atop a skyscraper, his broadcast suite is a centralised hexagonal room with glass walls all round. Through them, he can see adjoining control rooms, offices of his management, and the city to which he broadcasts every night. The cinematography is bound to aligning internal political machinations (framing his bosses' attempts to suppress his voice) with projected social agendas (symbolised by his gaze across the nightscape) as he speaks into the ever-present microphone. Both Barry's face and those of the station personnel are superimposed on each other, granting us a variety of lap-dissolves which simultaneously show talker and listener. This doubling of perspective figures Barry's speech as a collapse of monologue into dialogue: he mostly speaks in double senses, imparting something to a caller over the phone while inferring something else to his staff at the station.

Barry is at the centre of his own world – spatially, sonically and visually – as confirmed by the camera's circular arcs from his point of view. His ego is certainly not restrained, and his energy is such that it requires this bizarre glass cage to both release it as a hyper performance and to entrap it for dissemination. His hermetic world – part acoustic tomb, part idealistic incubator – gives Barry's voice its strength. When he speaks 'live' at a basketball game, his voice is acoustically blurred by the cavernous space; the audience is a restless din; they boo and hurl paper cups at him. Similarly, Barry's sense of self and his relationship to others is threatened whenever he steps out of his glass bubble. Conversely, when Barry lets the outside world into his control zone – the crazed fan, Kent (Michael Wincott) – Barry is confronted with the reality of those whom hitherto were an indistinct mass.

When the red light is illuminated as Barry is 'on air', he lights up his cigarette. The hyper-tactile sound of these energy flares indicates the dimensional warp we pass through to come into contact with Barry's psyche. Prophetically and tragically, Barry's death at the hands of an inflamed listener similarly blasts Barry 'off air'. Shot on the rooftop carpark of the station, he falls dead directly at the foot of the broadcast tower. As we survey the cityscape at night as a twinkling carpet of invisible listeners, a montage of their voices serves as a wake in remembrance of the voice of Barry Champlain – now a part of the ethesphere of talk radio.

Dir: Oliver Stone; **Prod:** A. Kitman Ho, Edward R. Pressman; **Scr:** Eric Bogosian, Oliver Stone; **DOP:** Robert Richardson; **Editor:** David Brenner, Joe Hutshing; **Score:** Stewart Copeland; **Sound Design:** Lon Bender, Wylie Stateman, **Main Cast:** Eric Bogosian, Ellen Greene, Leslie Hope, John C. McGinley, Alec Baldwin.

Taxi Driver
US, 1976 – 110 mins
Martin Scorsese

Set in a hot New York summer, *Taxi Driver* paints the town as seething, melting, hissing, steaming. Taxi cabs drive in slow motion through clusters of steam rising from manhole covers, suggesting the city is on the boil. Such a visual metaphor is apt and hard to misread. More complex is the way the music's orchestral score 'auralises' this metaphor.

Essentially a series of variations between two- and four-note oscillations, brass and string clusters inhale and sigh, replicating the breath of a spent body. That body is Vietnam veteran Travis Bickle (De Niro), an emotionally exhausted and psychologically drained being into whose empty hull has seeped the city's social sewer. His weary breath wheezing as if his lungs are full of mucus, Bickle is bent on flushing out that sewer like the street cleaners and the hosing-down of his own cab. He is a hollow shell who patrols the simmering city, as if the dark soil of its denizens has infected him. By extension, the orchestra often sounds like it is breathing through him, through the manholes, through the psychic being of the city and its inhabitants.

These melodic oscillations convey an incredible weight, always suggesting that they are not only playing notes, but modulating keys – symbolically dragging everything down with their own weight. This is not music of the airborne, the flighty, the ethereal, the transcendental: this is the sound of sinking, slowly and perceptibly. Mixed loudly in an onslaught of waves which envelop the image-track, the score's harmonia liquefies like glue rendered aqueous. Travis is slipping.

Skirting around and sometimes through this musical ooze is a cycling jazz motif that superficially holds the city as a hub to which jazz gravitates. But *Taxi Driver* utterly repels that clichéd son-image of the city as jazz melting pot. This New York is not sexy and saucy; it is asexual and acidic. The jazz motif's maudlin sax line is a sign of New Yorkers' emotional desperation and their displaced humanity. It connects Travis' yearning for an impossible affection with a WASP liberal campaigner's assistant Betsy (Shepherd), to Iris' (Foster) pathetic dance with her pimp Sport (Keitel) – in the latter, cued as a record played by Sport as he soft-talks Iris into submission. The theme's allusion to love is decrepit and acrimonious.

Just as the orchestra expresses energy welling from within the urban jungle and energy being drained to create Travis' existential containment, Travis expresses his self-transformation by working upon himself as a vessel. Figuratively, he becomes a gun: a sawn-off, body-primed double-barrel instrument through which the city's negative energy is compressed and fired. Travis refines his aim in the deafening din of the indoor gun range; those exact same sound effects appear on the soundtrack when he blasts Sport and his cohorts. These are psychic shots fired by a man so emptied that his penultimate actions ring with aching reverberant dissonance. As the orchestra overflows in a humoral bath of swirling harps and terse horns (phrasing the jazz theme), Travis lies like a spent cartridge. Once a man, then a gun, now no more than a human vocalising the sound of gunfire through his near-dying breath.

Dir: Martin Scorsese; **Prod:** Julia Phillips, Michael Phillips; **Scr:** Paul Schrader; **DOP:** Michael Chapman; **Editor:** Tom Rolf, Melvin Shapiro; **Score:** Bernard Herrmann; **Supervising Sound Effects Editor:** Frank E. Warner; **Main Cast:** Robert De Niro, Cybill Shepherd, Peter Boyle, Jodie Foster, Harvey Keitel.

Teenage Rebellion
US, 1967 – 81 mins
Norman T. Herman, Richard Lester

Deriving its pre-'mockumentary' form from 60s Italian exploitation documentaries like *Mondo Cane*, *Teenage Rebellion* chaotically strings together a hotchpotch of documentary footage of teenagers engaged in supposedly wild but ultimately banal activities around the world. The droll narrator's voiceover (by Burt Topper) attempts to make sense of the patchwork of jumbled camera work (including uncredited use of non-documentary films from Europe and Japan) bordered by po-faced faux-anthropological observations, each more a non sequitur than an analysis of any kind.

Such is the charm of *Teenage Rebellion*: it cannot help but cave in its own makeshift roof of rationalism as it pretends to explain, contextualise and qualify that which is beyond its scope. Never does the voiceover narration falter – despite the outrageous sociological assertions of its pseudo-beat poetry jive-talk. Never does it hint at its knowing inadequacy in moving beyond the pithy altruisms of its grand clichéd interpretations of life, ritual and the cosmos.

If the narrator is 'the voice of reason' in 'this crazy world in which we now live' (which he's not), then the score is a true-to-life snapshot of the subcultural sounds of teenagers at the time (which it's not). Tagging a slew of nondescript inept 'beat' sounds played by the type of session musicians who throughout the 60s desultorily mimicked rock and pop music they perceived to be well below their calibre, *Teenage Rebellion*'s soundtrack is its most potent anthropological document. Thin twangy guitar, stilted bongo drives, jazzy guitar lines, plus a range of non-rock instruments (harpsichord, trumpet, flute, castanets) are spread indiscriminately across the ad-hoc sequences of the film. The overall effect is one of indifferent 'rockzak', closer to James Last than Jimi Hendrix. The relationship between any musical passage and the scene it accompanies is arbitrary and almost irrelevant (the soundtrack album actually features excerpts of the film's voiceover narration – but paired with entirely different music). The sentiment essentially expressed by a 'documentary report' like *Teenage Rebellion* is that all teenager music is the same – despite the film claiming difference for its subject.

Teenage Rebellion's crazy spinning triangular configuration of scattered footage, fumbling voiceover and modular song placement constitutes a fascinating mode of soundtrack production whose audiovisual effect is greater than the sum of its parts. More openly televisual than formally cinematic, it casts music in a detached state, orbiting around the film but neither gravitating to any one point of appropriateness nor coming to rest at any single moment of significance – just like the rebellious teenager it is so bent on depicting.

Dir: Norman T. Herman, Richard Lester; **Prod:** Norman T. Herman; **Scr:** Norman T. Herman; **DOP:** various source documentary footage; **Editor:** uncredited; **Songs:** Dave Allen, Mike Curb.

Temptress Moon (*Feng yue*)
China, 1996 – 130 mins
Chen Kaige

Spanning the 1910s and 20s in China as British colonisation, opium trade
and revolutionary politics clash to give birth to China's new twentieth-
century world, *Temptress Moon* casts cycles of illumination over an
emotionally volatile constellation of three young adults whose childhood
circumstance fatally locks them into an obsessive orbit for years to come.
After arriving at the wealthy rural Pang estate to live with his older sister
Xiuyi (He) who has married the young lord Zheng (Zhou), Zhongliang
studies in between preparing their opium. Suffering emotional and sexual
abuse at their drug-addled hands, the young Zhongliang leaves for
Shanghai and grows into a cold and manipulative gigolo (Cheung). His
now-adult childhood friend Ruyi (Gong) takes over as head of the Pang
family and is aided by her distant relative Duanwu (Lin). Zhongliang's
Triad boss orders him to return home and bring Ruyi to Shanghai for
extortion of the Pang fortune. And so Zhongliang reunites his severed
contacts with devastating repercussions for everyone.

The use of this love triangle to illustrate the broader social changes is
a clearly announced agenda in *Temptress Moon*: the pre-credit text
outlines it, plus the film's 'generation in turmoil' theme is writ
handsomely large with stylistic grandeur. However, the film is unique in
the way it mobilises sound–image relationships to detail the bloodied
cauterised scarring that follows the impact of the social on the personal.
A particular audiovisual logic dictates this.

Very little camera work has the background in focus. Nearly always,
Zhongliang, Ruyi, Duanwu and others are posited in soft folds of space
and blurred contours of form. Their faces – sometimes only an angled
ear, the nape of a neck, a raised forehead – glow in sharp relief from
their settings. Yet, the sound is never partialised or hierarchically ordered
along such principles. Instead, sound is excessively greater than the visual
frame, forwarding not only that which is de-focused but also that which

is denied. This makes for a demanding and potent sound design whose weight, clarity and liveliness cuts across the mannered staging of the actors. Bats, geese, ducks, creaking oars, jumping fish, crickets, frogs, burning lanterns, firecrackers, clocks of all kinds, gongs, smashing plates, clinking cups, running taps, mah-jong cracks, kettle whistles, pigeons, bells, thunder, rain – the retinue of rural and urban 'auralities' are in hyper-focus and succulent grain.

This grants the film an aural fleshiness alluded to by Zhongliang, Ruyi and Duanwu's sexual awakenings and amorous shifts. Tied to the film's overreaching themes, their sexuality mutates from a rural earthy sensuality to urban taboo-shaking excitement. Zhongliang in particular embodies this transformation, and spreads it to the others when he returns, and when Ruyi and Duanwu come to Shanghai. The richness of sound – always timed to pregnant pauses and expectant heights – drowns the world of *Temptress Moon* in torrents of desire. A lurid love letter more than a stoic family tract, it audiovisually actualises the unspoken and the unspeakable which falls between the cracks of its epic structure.

Dir: Chen Kaige; **Prod:** Hsu Feng, Tong Cunlin; **Scr:** Chen Kaige, Shu Kei, Wang Anyi; **DOP:** Christopher Doyle; **Editor:** Pei Xiaonan; **Score:** Zhao Jiping; **Sound Design:** Lai Qizhen; **Main Cast:** Leslie Cheung, Li Gong, Kevin Lin, Caifei He.

(Next page) Temptress Moon: sound in excess of the visual frame

Tron
US, 1982 – 96 mins
Steve Lisberger

Tron's technologically rich tale of two cities – modern day Los Angeles
and the cyber world comprised of bits and bytes which at the time of the
film was radically transforming LA's entertainment industries –
constitutes a parable whose self-reflexivity spins into greater depths at
each thematic point. Its overreaching duality based on digital versions
and their analogues is openly declared through the exploits of all its key
characters existing in both real and virtual worlds, plus the many ways
images and sounds appear in actual and synthetic guise.

Alan Bradley (Boxleitner) and Kevin Flynn (Bridges) are game
designers with a passion for invention and creativity. Flynn is now an
embittered defector, since his designs were stolen by Ed Dillinger
(Warner), who created an empire for which Alan now works. Flynn teams
with Alan to break into Dillinger's offices and hack into the mainframe
computer to get data that proves Dillinger stole Flynn's designs, but in
the process of doing so Flynn is digitised into a computer world whose
logic of Users, Programs and Code takes on cosmic significance. Once
there, he encounters a matrix of similarities, simultaneities and simulacra
which uncannily replicate his 'outside' world of LA.

In its disavowal of verisimilitude, *Tron* stands as a landmark in
computer graphics. It interrogates simulation born of digital technologies
while refusing to create lifelike apparitions with those same technologies.
And while the past twenty years of regressive computer simulations
replay Renaissance-era optics combined with eighteenth-century musical
aesthetics, *Tron*'s sound design and film score seriously query the nature
of sound in the era of digital reproduction.

Retracing an avant-garde arc strung between Edgar Varèse and
Karlheinz Stockhausen, the score to *Tron* similarly stages the orchestra in
a hall of timbrel mirrors, using the orchestra to mimic itself, replicate
itself and confront itself. Mirroring the dual worlds which make up *Tron*'s

quantum landscape and textual mindspace, the score is comprised of synthesisers simulating orchestral instruments, and orchestral timbres simulating synthetic colourings. The weighting between the two is always fluid, as trills, rings, surges and decays will shimmer, never declaring a fixed identity, always suggesting that musical identity is simultaneous. This of course is echoed in *Tron*'s own story of simultaneity, as actions in each world impact the other in their precarious metaphysical balance. Similarly, the score is delicately caught between the material space of the 'users' and the virtual domain of the 'programs'.

Tron's sound likewise rejects naturalistic codes and invents a lexicon of effects, processes and sonic signifiers which postulate ways in which sound waves might occur in an immaterial dimension. Footsteps echo with pitches tuned to indicate difference in characters; interior and exterior acoustics are flattened and conflated due to the transitory nature of division between such spaces; echo and reverb take on psychological and emotional qualities more than reflecting physical phenomena; and mass and scale of sound are dependent on memory size, processor speed and CPU power. In its overall speculative rendering of an alternative existence ensnared by our codes of representation, *Tron* creates and generates a simulated world whose audiovisuality rewrites the coding and programming of cinema as a mimetic machine.

Dir: Steve Lisberger; **Prod:** Donald Kushner; **Scr:** Steven Lisberger, Bonnie MacBird; **DOP:** Bruce Logan; **Editor:** Jeff Gourson; **Score:** Wendy Carlos; **Sound Design:** Michael Fremmer, Gordon Ecker Jr, Wylie Stateman; **Special Sound Effects Design:** Frank Serafine; **Main Cast:** Jeff Bridges, Bruce Boxleitner, David Warner, Cindy Morgan.

Vagabonde (*Sans toit ni loi*)
France, 1985 – 105 mins
Agnès Varda

'Unmotivated action' is the central mystery to *Vagabonde*. What makes people do the things they do? How did they end up where they did? The vagabond of the title is Mona (Bonnaire), a young woman hitching rides around southern France, living in fields, shacking up with whoever she meets, stealing food when the moment presents itself. The film's narrative is appropriately transient: it opens with Mona's body discovered in a farm ditch, then follows a presumed narrative of her last few weeks based on casual interviews with those whose paths she crossed in the lead up to her undramatic death.

Five minutes into the film, you're following a story of which you know the outcome: this woman will die. As the story unfolds, one is brought into close proximity with the transient flow of life which governed Mona's philosophy and the conditions under which she existed. *Vagabonde*'s accompanying score of interlocked chamber instruments climbing over each other in serialist fashion marks Mona's actions and reactions with a haunting, stilling quality. A strange draining of pathos and seeping of affection fatally paints the young woman as a ghost – a fading being whose erasure is proportionately framed by people's wavering feelings towards her, and her response to their lack or surplus of affection. Emotional confusion reigns, as the music's atonality stalls one from committing to her character in one way or the other. Soliciting neither a stream of ennui nor a fissure of existentialism, *Vagabonde* creates a vacuum within which harmony is posited as a device deemed entirely incapable of coding the complexity of people's shifting emotional states. Like the unpredictably twisted and organically gnarled winter vines which spread across the realm where Mona will tragically freeze to death, the score obeys its own logic and existence beyond human endeavour.

Vagabonde: emancipated dissonance and parallel film scoring

While atonality is generally regarded as antithetical to humanist assertion, it can be so much more than the odd bump of chromatic progression to signify the absence of melodious accord. When its 'emancipation of dissonance' and liberation of wider harmonic possibilities are embraced by a film score, the core impulses of moments beyond the moral conventionalism of 'character motivation' can be captured and given great narrative depth. Part mystery, part tragedy, *Vagabonde*'s emancipated dissonance is tersely and unforgivingly matched to Mona's floating, detached, impulsive journey. Not a mode of enhancement, illustration, commentary or counterpoint, the score runs distinctly parallel to the film, creating an openly perplexing dialectic between music and action. *Vagabonde*'s meandering non-harmonic map makes one realise what little psychological territory we have covered in the musical characterisation of film scores.

Dir: Agnès Varda; **Prod:** Oury Milshtein; **Scr:** Agnès Varda; **DOP:** Patrick Blossier; **Editor:** Patricia Mazuy, Agnès Varda; **Score:** Joanna Bruzdowicz; **Songs:** Fred Chichin; **Sound:** Jean-Paul Mugel; **Main Cast:** Sandrine Bonnaire.

Videodrome
Canada, 1983 – 84 mins
David Cronenberg

Abstraction is key to the surfaces eroticised throughout *Videodrome*. Like faces in the clouds, visual textures and morphological parts in the film become uncanny representations of the apparent and the mysterious, the manifest and the latent. TV screens become skin; hands become guns; walls sweat like clay; lips wrap themselves around one like thighs; moist orifices are portals to mental dimensions. Always, one is caught between identification and disorientation, as abstraction swells and engorges the film's pornographic visage.

Abstraction performs similarly on *Videodrome*'s soundtrack. The film foregrounds 'breath' in both recognisable and abstracted states: from the synthetic noise of mock-human breath, to actual breath analogue-filtered, to the Synclavier simulating orchestral drones which historically symbolise vocal sighs and choral murmurs. Abstraction is encoded in the rendering of all sounds: one is continually aware of a 'humanness' that audibly strikes one as entirely inhuman. Here, the synthesiser is exploited for its queasy ability to render the human as a timbrelly pornographic presence while exempting it from physical performance.

The streaming and cascading waves of morphed orchestration in *Videodrome* paint a sonic abstraction of the schizophrenic media-being of the present, portrayed by Max Renn (Woods), whose journalist hunger for the shock of the new keeps him addicted not to any thing or topic, but simply to his own self-generating state of agitation and anxiety. Ripe for piercing the slick skin of any repressive traits – including his own – Max's interior state is thus less of fixed temperament and more of fluid potential. His personality is symbolised by the aura of digital and analogue textures in contrast, connoting clinical precision and rounded modulations respectively. In a progressively increasing state of being 'turned on', one simulates the other to create a schizophrenic vacillation between states of existence and perception matching Max's hallucinatory slippage. Hence, the score mutates between the heady erogenous heights of breaths dancing close to the eardrum – all whispers over salivated tongues and exhalations over sweat-beaded upper lips – and the faecal sensorial depths of rumbles from the stomach – all grumbling and gas displacements as the body's insides are realigned by exploratory activity. The latter realm is particularly noticeable in the sinewy orchestral lines which grow and cling to each other, forming unpredictable phalli, protrusions, and fissures of tonality.

Coated with *Videodrome*'s sono-scopic fix of media encoding, transference and transformation, bodily presences are as much sited by their mediated residue as their unmediated tactility. As cinema spends much care not to advance or promote the non-linguistic utterances of the mouth (breaths, gasps, drips, sniffles, groans, burps, etc.), it leaves pornography to be the sonic realm that celebrates and fetishises the mouth running at its pre-verbal fervour. Listening to *Videodrome* can be like hearing pornography – or, in accordance with the plot's themes – picking up interference deliberately being broadcast from an Other dimension. This is *Videodrome*'s defiantly erotic promulgation of the audiovisual grotesquerie which points to faces in clouds, lips upon ears, and vaginas within stomachs.

Dir: David Cronenberg; **Prod:** Claude Héroux; **Scr:** David Cronenberg; **DOP:** Mark Irwin; **Editor:** Ronald Sanders; **Score:** Howard Shore; **Sound:** Peter Burgess; **Main Cast:** James Woods, Sonja Smits, Deborah Harry, Peter Dvorsky, Leslie Carlson, Jack Creley.

Violated Angels (Okasareta hakui)
Japan, 1967 – 58 mins
Koji Wakamatsu

Violated Angels is an irrevocably compacted and resolutely stylised journey into the mind of a young and unnamed sexual psychopath (Kara) as he invades, terrorises and murders five nurses in their dormitory. Amorally leaving us deserted upon his psychological planet, the film scars us with its sounds and images.

The film's title shatters the screen to the sound of intensely loud gunshots. A photo-montage prelude follows, accompanied by a mournful electric organ, evoking the childlike playback of a theme from a roving food truck (heard often throughout Japan). Across this drooping theme, stills of 'our hero' are interspersed with pornographic images wrenched from magazines. The man appears to be consuming them; they also seem to be overwhelming him in a scopic onslaught.

Suddenly, we are at the ocean. It rages like an audiovisual wall of noise. The man fronts its massive swell – and fires a gun into it repeatedly. Those shots sonically aimed at us earlier are now being directed at the ocean's overwhelming power in a violently impotent act of sexual aggression, penetrating its liquefying bulk in repayment for the disenchanted dry-humping enacted in the preceding pornographic images of women with their silent mouths agape, falsely yearning for his manhood.

Cut to silence. A group of nurses sleep in their quarters – except for two engaged in sexual exploration. Their erotic murmuring and exhalation sparkles in the house's deadly quiet. An utterly strange growl reverberates in the distance – electronic, harsh, animalistic, inhuman. No one seems to notice it. A rattling noise outside: our prowling predator has wandered into their territory. The other nurses now awakened, they innocently yet mockingly invite him to watch the show . . .

Suddenly he fires a shot at one of the love-makers. Responding to this deadly sonic announcement, *Violated Angels*' morbid theatre of malicious acts now unfolds upon a blood-soaked tatami-stage, giving us a mix of Grand Guignol and kabuki. Gradually the nurses' massed cries subside and we notice only one voice: the dying convulsions of the shot nurse. All through this, the man watches the women, silently daring them to make a move. They become submissive to his glare, forced to audit the last gasp of their friend. Once she dies, they break into uncontrolled wailing.

This scenario is then played out in repeated modular form, often degenerating into nightmarish visions of all the women naked and moving in on him like an ocean of smothering flesh. Their crying, laughing and sobbing are processed into harshly echoic feedback-inducing sheets of post-human noise. His gunshots recurrently break into its oppressive sonic walls, just as he shot the ocean. The last nurse standing is the only one not to whimper. She speaks to him like a mother to a child, and sings a lullaby. Thus lulled to sleep, he becomes another naked body in the mandala pattern of the nurses' blood-soaked corpses. With his somnambulistic interment, the nurse disappears as the organ returns to extend her solo voice. *Violated Angels* is not for the faint of ear.

Dir: Koji Wakamatsu; **Prod:** Koji Wakamatsu; **Scr:** Masao Adachi, Juro Kara; **DOP:** Hideo Itoh; **Editor:** Fumio Tomita; **Score:** Koji Takamura; **Sound:** Shin Fukuda; **Main Cast:** Juro Kara, Shoko Kido, Keiko Koyanagi, Makiko Saegusa, Michiko Sakamoto, Kyoko Yayoi.

Way of the Dragon (*Meng Long Guojiang*)
Hong Kong, 1972 – 100 mins
Bruce Lee

Much laughter has been aimed at Hong Kong kung fu movies of the early 70s. Fortunately, the deafening roar of their active soundtracks drowns out the rabble of those who ridicule the films' unique audiovisuality. *Way of the Dragon* is not only a strong example of the genre, but also a transglobal commentary on the position held by Hong Kong action cinema at the time: wedged between Italian Westerns and Japanese samurai films. The film is set in Italy. Tang Lung (Lee) plays an awkward nephew who has come to help out his uncle's business in Rome. There he encounters a gang who extort his uncle, forcing Tang into an eventual gladiatorial conflict in the Colosseum with hired American killer, Colt (Norris).

A tawdry heroic pageant, *Way of the Dragon* would be dismissable if it weren't for the overwhelming physicality of the movie. Direction, choreography, performance, camera, editing and sound confer to represent one thing alone: the body of Bruce Lee. When Tang prepares for his battle at the Colosseum, we see in real time how thoroughly in control Lee is of his body, a percussive instrument in tune with itself, the result of him sounding his own body. Colt, meanwhile, manages some phantom blows into the air: all huff and bluff to Tang's scintillating crick and crack.

Percussivity and subjectivity form the subtextually aligned key to unlocking *Way of the Dragon*'s bodily soundtrack. It is partially derived from the sonic assault that accompanies Peking Opera's gymnastic feats, where cymbals and drums chart the energy transference at the heart of all *chi*-based martial arts. *Way of the Dragon* transposes that approach to scoring, and performs it not through a musical ensemble but through actual fight sequences. *Nanchuku* slaps and bone snaps, wood breaks and jaw cracks – all become sono-musical events timed to choreographed sequences, merging 'musicians' with 'actors' to form total sonic beings.

Way of the Dragon: the body as a percussive instrument in tune with itself

Often misread as being 'unnatural', the harsh percussivity of *Way of the Dragon* accords with its simulation of the subjective state of being hit. The hyper-tactile skin of the soundtrack is extended into it being itself a 'body' like Lee's. An ascetic 'narrowness' is discernible in its mono-dimensional mix where full volume level is continually maintained with no variation or modulation. The resulting 'weight' of the soundtrack again resembles Lee's body: a monolithic mass of muscle, its presence defined by its intensity.

The legacy of ta'i-chi is physically and theatrically foregrounded by Lee as he projects his body as an instrument for channelling its own energy and repelling energy directed at him. His howling voice symbolically and audibly conveys how he is conducting that energy through his body and into/onto others. Charged with pure physical adrenaline, he often lingers frozen after he has struck someone, as if still feeling the reverberant impact of his own strike, emblematic of *Way of the Dragon*'s holistic dissolution of sound into total physicality.

Dir: Bruce Lee; **Prod:** Raymond Chow, Bruce Lee; **Scr:** Bruce Lee; **DOP:** Tadashi Nishimoto, Ho Lang Shang; **Editor:** Chang Yao Chan; **Score:** Joseph Koo; **Sound:** Wang Ping; **Main Cast:** Bruce Lee, Nora Miao, Chuck Norris, Robert Wall, Ing-Sik Whang, Jon T. Benn.

Index

Page numbers in *italics* denote illustrations; those in **bold** indicate detailed analysis